THE CRASH OF NIMROD XV230

D1428519

H46 362 959 X

THE CRASH OF
NIMROD
XV230
A Victim's Perspective

TRISH KNIGHT

SilverWood

Published in 2012 by SilverWood Books, Bristol, BS1 4HJ
silverwoodbooks.co.uk

Copyright © Trish Knight 2012

The right of Trish Knight to be identified as the author of this work
has been asserted by her in accordance with the Copyright, Designs
and Patents Act 1988.

Paperback ISBN 978-1-78132-001-3
E-book ISBN 978-1-78132-008-2

The views expressed in this book are solely the opinion of the author.
All rights reserved. You may not copy, store, distribute, transmit,
reproduce or otherwise make available this publication (or any
part of it) in any form, or by any means (electronic, digital, optical,
mechanical, photocopying, recording or otherwise), without the
prior written permission of the copyright holder. Any person who
does any unauthorized act in relation to this publication may be
liable to criminal prosecution and civil claims for damages. The only
exception is by a reviewer, who may quote short excerpts in a review.

From the author:
My intention has been to tell a factual account of my experiences
surrounding the sudden death of my son; in doing so I have chosen to
omit as many other names as I felt able to, without detracting from
any of the facts. It is my account alone, and not the story of anyone
else. I sincerely hope that I have not upset or distressed anyone by
anything I have said, for that has not been my intention.

To Ben
1981 – 2006
"There's no such thing as luck!"

Contents

Andy and Ben Knight, July 2006, taken on a mobile phone

Foreword

On the morning of Sunday September 3rd 2006, United Kingdom newspaper headlines delivered the tragic news of the highest loss of life in a single incident to the British Armed Forces since the Falklands War in 1982.

'Carnage', 'I can see it burning in the fields', 'Fourteen lives cut off in their prime', 'The darkest day for our war heroes': All words employed by the headline writers in an attempt to convey a horror that most people cannot begin to imagine; the horror of being trapped in a burning aircraft, the de-pressurised cabin rapidly filling with smoke as you spiral 20,000ft in 90 seconds, whilst praying you will land safely.

The previous day, September 2nd 2006, fourteen men were on board the aircraft RAF Nimrod XV230 when it caught fire and exploded in the skies near Kandahar, Afghanistan. All fourteen souls on board were lost. This incident has become a footnote in history but it is also a date now etched forever in the memories of those affected by the tragedy.

As the eldest brother of Sgt Ben Knight, one of the fourteen men on board XV230 that day and referred to as 'A Band of Brothers' at the RAF Memorial Service, I still bear the scars of that fateful September day. In the immediate aftermath I could not find the space I needed in order to grieve fully, so five years on my grief still occasionally engulfs me; a kind of control mechanism holding back the overwhelming sea of emotion that lies deep within me. Feelings of guilt at being unable to help my little brother who I was raised to protect and look after; feelings of revulsion for those who failed in their duty to protect the crew of Nimrod XV230; and feelings too of pride and joy at being able to have known Ben for 25 years and of being able to call myself his brother. What I could not begin to comprehend in those early autumn days and weeks of September 2006 was the impact on those who had lost sons in the tragedy. Five years later, and now a father of two, I can say that I do not know how I would function if either of my children were lost in similar circumstances to my brother, or in fact in any circumstance.

You are about to read a mother's story, my mother's story, Ben's mother's story. But do not be fooled by the title of this book, for its contents portray a survivor's story of courage and determination and of a fight for justice. It is a story of a mother's bond with her child, a bond so strong that the urge to protect that child and to seek justice for that child extends way beyond the child's life. It offers a disturbing account of the actions that led to the loss of RAF Nimrod XV230 and a harrowing description of the consequences of those actions on the family of one of the fourteen men killed aboard it.

Miss you, Ben.

Andy Knight

From the Author

My youngest son, Ben, was killed aboard RAF Nimrod XV230 in the skies above Afghanistan on 2 September 2006. He was twenty-five-years-old. The aircraft caught fire after air-to-air refuelling and a 'Mayday' was declared. As the crew fought to control the blazing aircraft, in an attempt to reach Kandahar for an emergency landing, the aircraft exploded in mid-air. All fourteen crew on board were killed.

When Ben was growing up there were many occasions that warranted me wishing him 'good luck' – school exams or a game of squash to name but a few. However, Ben possessed a very logical mind and would always reply by saying, "There's no such thing as luck, Mother". He believed success depended upon knowledge learned; if he was unable to answer a question then he believed it was because he had not taken enough time to study the subject, and if he lost a game of squash it was because on the day his opponent was a better player. It was nothing to do with luck!

After the loss of Nimrod XV230, a small number of people criticized the intensity of our quest to establish what caused the aircraft to catch fire and explode, killing all fourteen men on board. Some said that those on board were simply 'unlucky' and that it was 'just an accident' and thought we should leave it at that. But there was no escaping Ben's words. For what happened aboard XV230 on that fateful Saturday was a result of a prior action. It had nothing to do with 'luck', and although it was an accident as opposed to a deliberate act, all accidents have a cause.

Since Ben's death the family has fought tirelessly to uncover the true state of the Nimrod fleet, and to obtain an element of justice for Ben by bringing those people responsible for his death and the loss of XV230 to account. In our opinion, our son was killed by incompetence, not by insurgents. The Ministry of Defence has accepted responsibility. *The Nimrod Review* by Charles Haddon-Cave QC, and commissioned by the Government, in my opinion, gave the illusion of justice but delivered none. Although we welcomed its findings, unfortunately it was left up to the families to pursue justice, if they so wished.

The publicity that surrounded the initial loss of XV230 was immense and immediately thrust us into the media spotlight. In an attempt to come to terms with everything that was happening to us at that time I began to keep a diary, for I didn't want such an horrific situation to eventually fade into obscurity. I recorded everything that happened to us on a daily basis for the first three months following Ben's death and continued to keep a weekly journal there afterwards including the mix-up of body parts and having a writ served upon me. I continued to record my feelings and our experiences as we struggled to live without Ben, at the same time as attempting to obtain an element of justice for him.

My reasons for writing this book are twofold. Firstly, I am Ben's mother and although Ben is dead he remains my child. My love for him has not diminished. A gross injustice has been inflicted upon my child and as his mother I have a duty to him to correct that injustice if at all possible. This book tells of our quest for justice. Secondly, our grandchildren have all been deprived of ever knowing their caring, fun-loving Uncle Ben, as they were all born after he was killed. Our eldest grandchild, Callum, was born just three months after Ben's death. So this book is for them, so they will eventually be able to read all about their wonderful Uncle Ben who was so cruelly taken from us all by a Government Department that, in my opinion, put cost before lives.

To our grandchildren: Callum, Charlie, and twins Poppy and Thomas.

Trish Knight
January 2012

1

Saturday 2 September 2006

Saturday 2 September 2006 started slowly and peacefully just like any other Saturday morning, but ended abruptly in a nightmare. I was pleased I had three days off work and enjoyed a quiet Saturday morning at home with my husband, Graham. In the afternoon we went shopping. The late summer sun gently warmed the day and everything in our lives felt normal. Unbeknown to us, that peace and normality was soon to be shattered. While I was enjoying a pleasant Saturday afternoon, the nightmare was already unfolding thousands of miles away on the other side of the world.

Gra and I had been out and arrived back at our home at four minutes to six in the late afternoon. I remember the exact time because it was just long enough for me to make myself a quick cup of coffee before the news began at the top of the hour. With my coffee made, I settled down on the sofa and switched the television on, ready to watch the news at six o'clock before I embarked on preparing the evening meal. I changed channels to Sky News and the first news item was a report that a helicopter had crashed in Afghanistan. I quickly reassured myself with the knowledge that our youngest son Ben, who was in the RAF, did not fly in a helicopter nor was he in Afghanistan; he was in Iraq, or so I understood. However, a few seconds later as I continued to watch, the newsreader said the latest information received by them had changed. They were now reporting that the crash involved a fixed-wing aircraft, thought to be a Hercules, but that the information had yet to be confirmed by the Ministry of Defence (MOD). Although Ben didn't fly in a Hercules, he did fly in a fixed-wing aircraft. I was beginning to feel really concerned and so was Gra, who had been watching the news with me. The information coming from the television seemed to be changing by the minute. It had started out as a helicopter crash and within seconds been updated to a fixed-wing Hercules. I just hoped beyond all hope that the aircraft type would not be changed again. We went through to the computer room and looked at the BBC World News online; to our horror it had changed and they were now reporting the crashed aircraft to be a Nimrod. Ben flew in a Nimrod.

By 6.30pm, Gra and I were beginning to panic. Gra was ashen-faced and distressed as neither of us wanted to believe what we were seeing and hearing. We hurried back into the lounge, desperate for more detail. As we did, Sky News gave out a helpline number for close relatives who were concerned. When it first appeared on the TV screen, we had not made a note of the number because we hadn't expected such a tragedy to involve us. You always think this sort of incident, sudden tragic accidents of headline news proportion, is something that happens to other people, not to you. In the same way you *know* you are going to die one day and so are your children, but you never really *believe* it will happen to you. It always feels as if it will happen to someone else. But that day, it happened to us.

As each minute went by our panic increased. We kept running between the television in the lounge and the computer room trying to catch the helpline number. I phoned our eldest son, Andy, and asked if he had seen the news. He said he had and believed the aircraft to be a helicopter. I corrected him immediately by saying it was a Nimrod that had crashed. He looked again on his computer while I was still on the phone to him, and this time he saw that it was a Nimrod that had crashed. I suddenly felt I needed the comfort and practicality of my eldest child and I asked him if he would come around to our house. Andy said he would come immediately. It was only a five minute drive from his house to ours, but while we were waiting for him to arrive, the helpline number eventually re-appeared at the bottom of the television screen and I frantically scribbled it down on a scrap of paper.

Referring to the collection of numbers as a 'helpline' is very misleading and thoughtless in my opinion. It is only natural to expect to receive help when you phone a helpline number. However, they were unable to offer me any help at all. All they did was take details from *me*, when what I so desperately needed was details from *them*. I wanted to hear that Ben was alive and ok, and that he was not on the aircraft that had crashed. At the time, and in the suffocating state I was in, it didn't seem an unrealistic request to want to know that my son was safe. Instead, they asked me for the details of the relative I was concerned about, wanting to know his name, rank, squadron and military number. I hurriedly provided them with the information they required. They then asked for my name, address and telephone number, said 'thank you' and that was it. They didn't help in any way. I wanted them to confirm that Ben, my Ben, was safe. It would not have taken them many minutes to do so. I was frantic and confused. I wanted to shout at them… to say to them they could not leave me in this limbo… they had to tell me Ben was safe. After all, that was what they were there for, wasn't it? To 'help'? But they were unable to. They were a helpline without any help to offer.

In desperation, we returned to the computer and continued to search the internet for more details about the crash, but to no avail. By now it was about 7.00pm and Andy had already arrived. Gra and I didn't know what to do. Looking back at that evening five years later, I don't know why we didn't telephone Ben's home number in Inverness, but we were in a state of fear and panic and our normal thought processes had completely collapsed. I asked Andy if he would go and see his younger brother, Matt, and his partner, to find out if they had heard about the crash – and if they had, to come back and let me know how they were coping with the unfolding events. They lived a short distance away from us and were expecting their first child in December 2006. I insisted to Andy that he was to come straight back after he had spoken with them and he promised he would.

Andy had been gone for about fifteen to twenty minutes when the doorbell rang. I immediately thought it was him returning from his brother's house and said so to Gra. I rushed to the door and opened it –

And the nightmare engulfed me. There on the doorstep stood two RAF personnel. A lady and a man, both in full RAF uniform. I took one look at them and shouted, 'No!' My head shook from side to side automatically as the word 'no' kept running through my mind. I stepped backwards into the hallway in an attempt to retreat from the devastating reality that stood before me. They didn't need to say anything; I knew what their presence meant.

They asked me to confirm who I was, apologised for their presence and asked to come in. My mind was racing; I didn't want them in my house. I thought if I didn't let them into the house then they couldn't tell me anything. They wouldn't be able to tell me what I knew they were going to.

Gra heard me shout 'no' and dashed into the hall to see what was happening. He put his arms around me as I instantly became a physical and mental wreck. I let them into the house because I was incapable of doing anything else. As they walked into the hallway, they said how sorry they were that they had to inform us that Ben was 'missing, presumed dead'. That was the worst moment of our lives. From that evening, after the few seconds it took me to open the front door to the two RAF personnel, our lives were changed forever.

To this day I don't know how I survived that Saturday evening and the definitive knock on the door.

Gra and I moved into the lounge with our two unwanted RAF visitors following behind. We sat down on the sofa, both of us totally bewildered. Andy returned from his brother's house shortly after the two RAF personnel arrived. As he entered the lounge, the expression on his face changed as he realised the significance of the visitors. As they turned to speak to him, Gra confirmed to Andy that Ben was dead and asked what were we going to do without him. I cannot remember what I said to Andy. There are times when my mind appears to have totally blanked out some memories, perhaps as a defence mechanism. Other memories of those first few hours of realisation, however, are as clear to me today as if they had happened only yesterday. As Andy tried to make sense of the awful situation, I asked the impossible of him: I asked him if he would return to his brother's house and break the dreadful news that Ben was dead. Tearfully, he retraced his steps back to their house, informed Matt and his partner of the devastating news before returning to us again.

Over the next few hours, we learned how 'missing, presumed dead' is just a phrase the military use. Ben was dead from the moment the aircraft exploded, but until bodies/parts have been recovered, they are technically still 'missing'.

Gra and I spent the rest of that evening in a state of disbelief and in tears; the tears came from hearts that were beating out their grief. The RAF lady, who sat trying to comfort us, was a Padre from RAF Lyneham. I don't know the military rank of the man, but I noticed how polite he was.

He wouldn't sit down until he was invited to do so. During the course of that unbearable evening, he left the room on numerous occasions to make telephone calls in private. Each time he returned to our lounge, he again wouldn't sit down until he had been formally invited. It is strange the idiosyncrasies one notices at such a devastating time and I found myself feeling a little sorry for him. However, as that very long and unbearable evening wore on, what I had first thought of as 'politeness' I began to see as an irritant. Outside, sitting in a smart vehicle, was the driver who had driven the two RAF personnel to our house and whose job it was to sit there all evening and late into the night until he was required to drive them back to the airbase.

I was concerned about Ben's fiancée and wanted to know whether she had been told yet. The very polite RAF gentleman made a few more phone calls then confirmed, 'Yes, she has been told.' I wanted to talk to her. I thought that if I could just talk to her and say, 'It's a mistake, it can't be true' then somehow it wouldn't be true. I can't remember whether I did talk to her that evening, I would have thought I did, but I have no recollection of a conversation. There were other telephone calls made by Gra and myself that evening to close family, informing them of Ben's death, but neither of us can recall the exact contents of those calls and to whom they were made. Shock crept quietly in that evening and stole certain memories from us.

Understandably, we wanted to know what had happened to the aircraft and what had caused the accident. The RAF Padre, who by this time had told us to call her Ruth, told us what little detail she could. That there had been a fire on the aircraft, then an explosion and that all fourteen men on board were 'missing, presumed dead'. Ruth and her colleague stayed with us late into the night. They sat and listened to our distress, offering comfort where they could, but we were distraught and found the enormity of what had happened almost impossible to bear. Gra wanted us to drive to Inverness that evening, but we were certainly in no fit state to do so. After much dissuasion from Ruth and myself, he eventually agreed that such a drive in his utterly distressed state was not a good idea. Our two unwanted RAF messengers then began to make arrangements for us to travel to Inverness and RAF Kinloss the following day.

Gra does not like flying; he has flown on about six occasions, but finding the experience more difficult to cope with each time, he now avoids travelling by air. Other methods of travel can be quite expensive and more time-consuming but it is something I have had to learn to accept. Ben, however, loved flying and chose it as a career. It seemed a strange contrast between father and son – one loving flying and the other loathing it.

Ruth and her colleague remained with us throughout that torturous evening and did not leave our house until about 11.45pm, by which time they had arranged for a car to take us to the north of Scotland the following day. Our eldest son, Andy, said he would stay with us that night and help us pack some clothes for our long journey to Inverness. We put a few clothes in a suitcase, ready for our early start the following day, but we were in a dreadful state of disbelief and didn't achieve much. By 2.00am we lay on our beds wide awake, wanting to be alone but waiting for sleep to arrive.

After a couple of hours of restless sleep, we awoke at 6.15 on Sunday morning. For a few short moments on waking, Gra and I found ourselves questioning whether the events of yesterday evening really had taken place. Ben could not be dead; he was so loud, cheeky, outgoing and many other adjectives but certainly not 'dead'. 'Dead' was something that happened to other people, to other families, but certainly not us, not to our family! Ben was our youngest child and children aren't supposed to die before their parents. That just wasn't how life was meant to be. But within seconds we had to accept the awful events of yesterday were indeed real.

After I had dressed, I went next door to our neighbours and explained, as best I could, what had happened the previous evening. In between tears, I informed them that we would be away for at least a couple of weeks. While I was there, Andy made arrangements for someone to look after our two dogs. I had no thought of breakfast; the pain that had developed in my stomach truly filled me to the brim, and the thought of putting any food into my mouth gave me a feeling of nausea. At 8.50am the transport the two RAF personnel had organized the evening before arrived. It consisted of two drivers, one lady and one man, and a Ford Galaxy. We hugged Andy and said our goodbyes, climbed into the Galaxy and left for the north of Scotland. We didn't know what we would do or what would happen once we arrived, but we both knew we just had to be there, where Ben had lived and where we had shared many good times with him. Andy was going to make some necessary telephone calls and then drive up to Scotland later on Sunday with his brother, Matt.

The two drivers from RAF Lyneham informed us that they were going to drive us as far as Carlisle, then we were to change vehicles and continue our journey north with a driver that had been despatched from RAF Kinloss. The journey from Somerset to Inverness is a long one, but we usually enjoyed it. The further north you travel, the more magnificent the scenery becomes. The volume of traffic gradually decreases as the mountains take control and rise above all else, except for the rolling clouds and blue skies. However, the journey that Sunday was one of continuous disbelief and despair. We had great difficulty understanding the situation that had been thrust upon us. I thought if I could just arrive at Inverness then someone would tell me it was all a mistake and that Ben wasn't dead after all.

Gra and I sat in silence for most of the long journey, for there seemed little to say. No amount of words could put right what had taken place the day before. A couple of times we stopped at the motorway services for a toilet break and a drink, but neither Gra nor I felt the need to eat or drink; disbelief and shock took care of our hunger and thirst. During the process of arranging the transport the evening before, I had panicked and said I didn't want to stop at motorway services and have to walk through crowds of raucous and excited travellers. I felt I didn't want to see or be seen by happy and contented people going about their daily life – not now that my life had been brutally torn from me. I wanted to be wrapped in a dark blanket and put in a corner of a room until this nightmare realised it had targeted the wrong person and moved on.

I'd been reassured on Saturday evening that we wouldn't stop at any motorway services, but I guess the drivers hadn't been informed of this, and anyway it would have been extremely difficult to spend the whole journey trying to locate alternative rest areas.

When we reached our first scheduled service break, a feeling of panic suddenly ran through my entire body and I didn't think I could survive outside of the car. I was not ready to leave the security of the vehicle and face the outside world with all its energy and exuberance. I just couldn't do it. The drivers seemed to understand, so Gra and I sat silently in the car with only our thoughts, while they took a statutory break. It was not until early afternoon, and at a subsequent motorway service stop, that I asked the female driver if she could walk to the toilets with me. I didn't feel I was physically capable of making the journey alone, nor did I want to have to pass the newspaper stands. Unfortunately, we had no choice but to walk through the shop area on our way to the toilets and I suddenly came face to face with the newspaper billboards. They showed a picture of a Nimrod and talked of the crash. Across the front of every Sunday newspaper was a headline about the crashed Nimrod. Some of the newspapers called it a 'spy plane'. I gasped and pointed out the headlines to the female driver who was with me but she quickly hurried me along. It seemed that everywhere I looked there were pictures printed of Ben and some of the crew. The newspapers were saying Ben was dead, but I had great difficulty understanding how that could be. Ben could not be dead, he was only twenty-five and was full of life – and he was our child. I know it's a tired cliché but your children aren't supposed to die before you. It was all very surreal. Ben was not supposed to be dead. All the newspapers were running the story confirming the crash, but I still couldn't understand how this could be happening to me... and to us as a family. I thought that if only the newspapers would stop saying he was dead, then maybe he wouldn't *be* dead.

The whole situation was a most horrendous experience and truly was a living nightmare.

Gra didn't move far from the relative safety of the car, apart from to have a cigarette, until mid afternoon. Like me, he didn't want to be confronted with all the newspaper photos of Ben, the crew, and the headlines. Gra told me some months later that the 'smoking kills' warning on the back of his cigarette packet taunted him during that long, sad drive to Inverness as he struggled to understand 'why Ben and not me?' Gra had smoked all his life and Ben had never smoked; yet Ben was dead and Gra was alive.

At Carlisle, we changed vehicles and drivers. We now had one male driver to take us to Inverness. When we climbed in the vehicle the radio was playing. Gra asked the driver if he would turn the radio off, as it was inappropriate given the circumstances. I understood the reason for his request but it left an even more uncomfortable atmosphere in the car. As we drove nearer to Scotland and over the border, I didn't think that I would ever be able to visit Scotland again. Usually, Gra and I both enjoyed travelling north to stay with Ben and thought the scenery was exquisite, but now I really didn't think I would ever be able to return once this final nightmare journey was completed. I watched solemnly out of the window as lochs and mountains passed us by, and with each new view, I silently bid a final farewell to Scotland.

As we got nearer to our destination, I received a text from Ben's fiancée asking how far we had travelled and what time we might arrive. I immediately texted her back, yet again saying I could not believe this was happening to us. She asked when Andy and Matt would be arriving and I told her they expected to arrive at about midnight. As we reached the crest of the final hill, we could see the highland city of Inverness stretching out below with the Moray Firth extending out into the North Sea. The other side of the Moray Firth sat the Black Isle, beyond that the lonely mountains of the far North. Normally, this heralds the end of our long journey. However, this time it meant the start of a new journey – one that would test us to our limits and take all our energy to see it through.

We arrived at Inverness at about 8.00pm, and as I stood outside Ben's house, I cried. I cried for all his lost aspirations and dreams. I cried because he would never see his brand new house again, the house he was so proud to have bought only eight months ago with its still unfinished back garden. And I cried for myself, for the heartache and agony, despair and desolation that I felt now Ben was no longer in my life.

As we walked into the house, Ben's fiancée and I hugged each other and I cried again. She introduced us to her Visiting Officer (VO) and also to our VO, both of whom were RAF personnel. They informed us that they were there to help and support us in whatever way they could, for as long as we needed them. We bombarded our VO with question after question that Sunday evening as we sat and talked for hours and hours late into the night.

Andy and Matt arrived in Inverness around midnight. They'd taken turns driving up, and had covered the distance in a shorter time than we had.

When that very long day eventually came to an end, somehow Ben was still dead... and I was unable to understand how and why this unbelievable and unimaginable horror had befallen us.

2

Ben

I first met Graham when I was a determined teenager, aged nineteen, and he was a twenty-year-old aspiring part-time bass guitarist. Of course, I didn't know then that we would become husband and wife and go on to celebrate thirty-eight years of married life. At the time of our first meeting, I was working as a student nursery nurse in a large children's home situated in the small, quiet Warwickshire market town of Coleshill, which was where he lived. By day, he worked in his father's plumbing and building business and lived at home with his parents. By night, he was out with the band getting gigs where they could.

We met at the end of a cold November in 1972 and he proposed to me just three weeks later – the week before Christmas. By the end of March the following year, we were a married couple. Looking back, I can understand how our relationship could be described by some as 'love at first sight', but at the time I don't think either of us thought that way; we were just young and wanting to enjoy ourselves. I'm sure most of our friends didn't expect the relationship to last, as it certainly fit into the whirlwind romance category, but here we are still together after thirty-eight years.

A month after our marriage, we moved to the comparative quietness of Cornwall to live and work for a year, because that was just the sort of thing you did in the 70s. We lived and worked in the sunny holiday town of Newquay for the first six months and moved to the quaint little fishing village of Mevagissey for the latter six months, where at high spring tides the sea would gently lap around the sand bags that we positioned with great care outside our front door. We didn't realise it at the time but when we were living in Newquay we were just eight miles from RAF St Mawgan, where the Nimrod aircraft were then based, and on which our youngest child Ben – as yet unborn – would be killed.

The first Nimrod to enter operational service with the RAF was Nimrod XV230, delivered to RAF St Mawgan on 2 October 1969. It may well have flown over our heads during that carefree summer in Cornwall, but if it did we were oblivious to the fact; we were too busy enjoying our young lives, our freedom and planning our future together – the three things Ben had taken from him by that very same aircraft. It would be thirty-three years before the significance of Nimrod XV230 would become brutally apparent to us.

In April 1974, we relocated and settled in the old market town of Bridgwater, Somerset. Newquay was a carefree place to be in the dizzy summer months of our youth, but when the summer surrendered to autumn and the holidaymakers returned to the normality of their own homes, we found the town very quiet and a feeling of isolation set in. I believe the town is very different nowadays and has developed into an all year round resort.

We didn't plan on spending the rest of our lives in rural Somerset but somehow that was what happened. Our first child, Andrew (Andy), was born in November 1974. At the time, Gra was working as a chef at the large general hospital in Taunton whilst attending college to gain the required catering qualifications. Through choice it was five years later before we had our next son, Matthew (Matt). By this time, Gra had progressed in his chosen career and was a chef in the local maternity hospital, so he cooked all my meals whilst I was in hospital having Matthew. It also meant he was on hand for flexible visiting, although the phrase had yet to be invented. We always wanted three children, irrelevant of whether they be male or female, and decided not to leave it so long next time. In fact, we decided to do quite the reverse and, rather than wait the five years we had between Andy and Matt, our youngest son, Benjamin (Ben), was born just sixteen months after Matt.

Ben was born premature, expected in the March of 1981 but arriving at the end of January. His birth took place in the same hospital in which our other two children had been born, and where Gra still worked as a chef. It was only a very small hospital with about fifteen beds, and the staff later told Gra that had I been someone else, they would probably have sent me to the general hospital to give birth. Because Ben was premature, he experienced breathing problems when he was born and needed to go into an incubator. The hospital had been given an incubator some months earlier, but until Ben was born, they hadn't needed to use it; now they had to set about wiping it down with sterilising liquid and reading the instruction manual.

The use of the incubator was such an event at the small maternity home that an article was written in the local paper about it. It read:

> *Friends see Benefit of their Work*
> *Friends of Bridgwater Hospital held their monthly meeting at the Mary Stanley Maternity Home... Members were told that a previous gift of a heated incubator had been put to good use in transporting a premature baby to the maternity unit at Musgrove Park Hospital. The baby, now making good progress back at Bridgwater, was admired by the visitors.*

It was somewhat uncanny that Ben's life began and

ended with articles in the newspaper about him. It portrayed a style of neatness, a complete circle, to his life.

Because Ben was premature, we were moved to a special care baby unit at a hospital in Taunton and had to stay in hospital longer than expected. We were confined in the sterile world of the hospital environment for three long weeks, leaving Gra to look after Andy and Matt. I will never forget the alarming words of the nursing staff when I was eventually allowed to leave hospital, cradling our precious addition to the family in my arms. They informed me that Ben 'would always be a bit behind' in his learning capabilities compared to other children of his age, due to his prematurity. However, their unpalatable prognosis proved to be totally incorrect as Ben went on to become a member of Mensa when he was only eight-years-old; at the time he was one of their youngest members.

Ben's premature and totally unexpected start in life took Gra and I by surprise and seemed to lay the foundation for how he was to live the rest of his life. He always strived to surprise us with his exploits, but as he grew up, his need to surprise became so predictable that, to his annoyance, we ceased to be surprised at his actions – apart from the ultimate one which took us totally by surprise and absolutely devastated us.

Ben was fifteen-months-old when the Falklands War began in early April of 1982. Margaret Thatcher was the Conservative Prime Minister who led a willing nation into a bloody war that would have a huge impact on many service personnel and their families. Of course, we didn't know it then, but we were destined to become one of those families; however, the significance would not become apparent until after Ben's death. The Falklands War led to an Urgent Operational Requirement (UOR) to equip RAF Nimrods with air-to-air (AAR) refuelling capabilities. In layman's terms, the Nimrod aircraft was needed to patrol the Falklands but didn't have the fuel tank capacity to fly from Britain to the Falklands without refuelling, therefore, it was modified to allow AAR refuelling to take place. The modification work was hastily completed in record time. It is quite remarkable to be able to trace a pattern of events in the way that we have been able to, but we now know that the fitting of AAR capabilities in 1982 was the beginning of a sequence of events that would eventually lead to Ben's death.

At the age of five, Ben attended the local junior school which was a short walk from our home; it was the same school that both his older brothers attended. His teachers said his schoolwork was excellent, although a little untidy, and he also excelled in sports.

While Ben was still at junior school, Gra and Andy both played squash at the local sports centre, with Andy taking part in many squash competitions around the county. From an early age, Ben was familiar with the many squash courts and tournaments around the county as he and the rest of the family accompanied Andy to his many matches, and it seemed inevitable that Ben would eventually follow that route. Gra enrolled Ben in the junior squash club when he was nine-years-old and, as expected, it soon became clear he was an outstanding player for his age. His enthusiasm and ability for the game was there for all to see, and he began playing for the Somerset Under-12s squash team when he was ten-years-old. We continued to travel around the South West of England this time, taking Ben to the many competitions and training events he would sign up for. Although he went on to win many competitions, he always accepted that there were going to be people who could beat him at a game of squash. When he reached his teens, he began coaching the younger children in the squash club and thoroughly enjoyed his time there.

When he reached eleven years of age, Ben left the junior

school and moved to the local senior school, East Bridgwater Community School. It was here that, due to his academic achievements, his infectious zest for life and his ability to inspire others, he was rewarded with the status of Head Boy in his final year, a position he fully embraced.

In May 1996, Ben took part in the Ten Tors Challenge, which his school participated in each year, and he was delighted to be chosen as Team Leader. The Ten Tors Expedition is an annual hiking weekend across Dartmoor National Park and takes place in early May. About 2,400 young people train for many months for the event, which is organized by volunteers and helped by the British Army.

On the weekend of the event that year, Gra and Matt and I travelled down to Exeter on the Saturday evening and stopped overnight so we could get to Dartmoor early on the Sunday morning to see Ben's six-man team come over the finish line. When we awoke on the Sunday morning, we switched on the television in the hotel room to hear the newsreader announcing a major emergency on Dartmoor. Apparently, there had been deep snow and torrential rain falling for many hours, causing the event to finally be cancelled as the blizzard quickly swallowed up the moors. Some of the children taking part were being airlifted off the moors, and many of them had various degrees of hyperthermia. Naturally, we were worried and rang the emergency number we had been given prior to the start of the weekend. We were told by a friend of Ben's that he was very disappointed that, after having hiked so far on the first day, they would have to retrace their steps on the second day back to one of the army camps. We were later informed by another of Ben's friends that he'd told them at the camp he would only leave the moor and abandon the race as long as the organisers agreed to award them the medal for finishing.

Because of the unusual situation caused by the freak weather conditions of heavy snow in May, it was agreed that the team would be awarded a medal. It was the first time in the event's history that it had to be cancelled. During the event, Ben had lost his waterproof trousers and, believing them to have fallen out of his rucksack onto the moor, he had walked for what seemed like miles with just an ordinary pair of trousers, and one fleece on his top half. Later, as the team went through the scrutiny process at the end of the race, Ben found that his waterproofs were stuffed right at the bottom of his bag and that he hadn't lost them after all!

Gra had changed careers in the mid-Eighties and had decided to train as a Registered Mental Nurse. I began work as a civil servant in September of 1989, and life appeared to be going along comfortably. This all changed in November 1997 when Gra suddenly became seriously ill. He was rushed into hospital, as his body went into shock, and the following day underwent an emergency operation. He had peritonitis, septicaemia and had his appendix and a length of his bowel removed. He also had to have an emergency colostomy, which was reversed in another operation six months later.

When I telephoned the hospital following what I understood was just an 'ordinary exploratory operation', I was informed by the nursing staff that, instead of him being returned to the ward after the operation, he had been taken to Intensive Care. I was shocked and distressed by this news. When I asked if he would live, they replied they did not know, reminding me that he had been extremely poorly prior to the operation, and although they hoped he would survive, it was really far too early to say whether he would.

The week Gra was taken into hospital, Ben was away on an outdoor pursuit college course near London. I had an agonizing time trying to decide if I should recall Ben from his course or not. If Gra was going to die, then Ben should certainly have the opportunity to see and speak to his father for one last time. Alternatively, I didn't want to distress Ben anymore than was necessary, and if Gra survived, then Ben could see him at the weekend when he returned home.

I telephoned Ben on the Wednesday evening, the day following Gra's operation, and let him know that his dad had needed to go into to hospital because he had a poorly stomach. I explained that he'd had an operation, but that he was ok. Ben listened to what I had to say, then excitedly began telling me what a good time they were having, but that he had fallen down on the artificial ski slope and broken one of his fingers. I told him to take care, enjoy the remainder of his course and we would see him on Friday evening when he was due back home. All I could do then was to pray that I had made the right decision by choosing not to let Ben know about the true situation regarding his father's health.

Gra's illness had a profound effect on Ben, who was a couple months off being seventeen at the time. When he returned home, he put off visiting his father for a couple of days because he didn't want to see his dad with all the tubes and wires trailing from his near lifeless body. When he did visit him, it was a great shock to Ben to see how ill his dad looked, and on the way home in the car afterwards, Ben sat alone on the back seat and cried. Ben's intense reaction to Gra being ill was a bit of a surprise to us. Yes, we understood that he would be upset, but he took it exceptionally hard.

In the January of 1998, Ben wrote the following words on his computer. He never showed it to us, but two years after he joined the RAF, we found it and printed a copy. He eventually knew we had read it, but with the added maturity that comes with age he could accept that fact.

Billions of stars float endlessly in the void of space, just waiting for a dreamer, someone who will grasp them with both hands and hang on as if their very life depends upon it, as if it was a necessity like air or food... Everyone taking a different life route. How am I supposed to know which one to take? It might be the wrong one. I used to know, before Dad was ill, I was on a road and prepared to follow it for eternity. I thought it was the right way, to me it was the only way.

I don't think anyone ever truly knows where they are going, they just have a feeling in their heart and ride that feeling until it burns out. Mine Did!

I have always believed that to find true direction you must push the physical limits of the body, push them until you can't take anymore, and go on. When the wind is howling at your back and the mountains defying you, when all of hell is upon you trying to bring you down, then you find out who you are.

I felt so helpless, so guilty that I wasn't there, so angry that I could not face to see him, lying there, tubes hanging out like he was a machine, for two weeks my father died, each night we would visit a shadow of my dad. These past weeks he's been a father again, he's teaching me to drive, that's who he is. A teacher, a teacher whose job wasn't done, how dare he leave, he hasn't finished, what am I supposed to do, teach myself. I don't know how to do anything without him!

If dad died I don't think I could go on, he is my soul,
He is the hand that rocks me as a babe,
He is the sun that warms me on a summer's day as a child,
He is the blanket that protects me at night,
He is the air I breathe every second of the day,

He is the determination that drives me,
He is the strength that pushes me forward,
He is my heart… without him there is nothing.

We are grateful to have these written thoughts by Ben but they are also very upsetting.

As Ben grew up, he became even more adventurous and, when he was seventeen, he and his then girlfriend went off to the USA and Canada for a month long touring holiday. Ben arranged all the travel and accommodation himself via the internet at a time when the internet was still a relatively new phenomenon.

Shortly after they returned from the holiday, his girlfriend went away to university and she ended their relationship. Ben was very upset and went to visit her at university in an attempt to win her back; sadly for Ben, he didn't succeed. Gra's illness the previous year and now this rejection by his girlfriend seemed to take its toll on Ben and he appeared to 'lose his way' to a certain extent career-wise. He eventually settled into work at the sports centre as a leisure assistant, which usually involved working evenings and weekends. At the weekend, he would quite often telephone me at home and ask what we were having for dinner. If he liked the sound of what the meal was, he would ask me to put some on a plate and deliver it to the sports centre for him, together with a newspaper. If he preferred something else to eat, he would ask me to make that particular dish and take it to him. In such situations, his vivacious wit and enthusiastic pleadings would win me over, and of course for 'my Ben', I usually succumbed to his demands.

While the children were young and growing up, we usually took them abroad each summer for a holiday, travelling by coach, train or aeroplane. Even as a child, Ben's preferred option of travel was by plane. If we were fortunate enough to be allocated a seat next to a window,

Ben would sit on the edge of his seat, his exuberance clear for all to see, as he looked out of the small window across the fluffy white clouds and the distant landscape in absolute awe. Then, in 1986, the film *Top Gun* was released and Ben was mesmerized by a combination of action, symbolism, stunning photography and powerful music. We first purchased the film on video, but Ben played it so often that the tape wore out. As DVDs began to creep into existence, that became our next choice of play. *Top Gun* became Ben's favourite film and, as he had a very good memory, he soon knew almost every sentence of the film. As he grew up, he was able to recite any part in order to suit his situation.

Until the age of eleven, Ben had wanted to be an astronaut. However, he soon seemed to realise that it was highly unlikely he would achieve that aim and altered his goal to joining the Royal Air Force and flying. His holiday to America and Canada just compounded his love of flying, and on his return, he started talking about having flying lessons. One afternoon, when he was aged seventeen, he and a close friend of his drove to a remote flying school in Somerset to enquire about flying lessons. Shortly after his death, that friend recalled to us how keen Ben had been to learn to fly but that he was shocked when he learnt how much it would cost him to have private lessons. She felt it was that afternoon drive to the flying school that spurred him on into filling out the RAF application form. Ben later introduced this same friend to another friend of his and they became boyfriend and girlfriend; I understand they are now married. This second friend stayed at our house on a couple of occasions and he and Ben discussed their futures, as friends do. He emphasized to Ben the huge cost of private flying lessons and told him if he wanted a career in flying, then he should join the RAF. I have absolutely no problem with the advice he gave Ben, for he put Ben back on track after being in a state of limbo for about twelve months following his father's illness and a lost relationship. Ben eventually decided to follow his dream and we were very happy for him.

So it was that Ben eventually went to the RAF Recruiting Office in Exeter and obtained the necessary application forms. The process was a long one and required Ben to travel to RAF Cranwell in Lincolnshire for a number of interviews and tests. The cost of travelling to RAF Cranwell for the interviews was paid for by the RAF. They would send him the required paperwork and Ben would go along to the railway station and get his ticket. Each ticket stated which carriage he would be travelling in, and the number of the seat that had been allocated to him.

On 17 October 2000, Ben had one of the interviews at RAF Cranwell arranged. He showed us the train ticket prior to travelling so we knew the details of his travel that day. He would be going by train to London, then catching another train at 12.10pm from Kings Cross to Leeds, which would take him on to Lincolnshire. As Gra worked from home, he turned on the television at 1pm to watch Sky News while he had a break and some lunch. Suddenly, a news flash appeared along the bottom of the screen stating that the 12.10pm train from Kings Cross Station going to Leeds had crashed at 12.23pm near Hatfield. The newsreader added that it was understood there had been some deaths. Gra was suddenly in a state of panic and tried to recall Ben's carriage number and seat number. He quickly rang Ben's mobile phone but was greeted by the message, "This person's phone is turned off, please try later or send a text."

Not knowing what to do next, Gra phoned me at work and told me what had happened. He said he was sure that one of the overturned carriages was the one Ben had a ticket for, and that he'd tried calling him but his phone was turned off. He asked if I could come home from work and said he would drive into town and collect me. At work I hurriedly explained what had happened and asked permission to go home, which of course was agreed.

When I arrived home, I switched the television news on and realised immediately I had to confirm Gra's fears, telling him the train that had crashed was the one Ben was due to travel on. What was even worse was that the carriage lying on its side and the one believed by the television media to have fatalities in it was the carriage number that Ben held a ticket for. A helpline number had been given out and was scrolling across the bottom of the screen, so I quickly scribbled it down on a piece of paper and proceeded to phone it. However, they were not able to offer any help, as their title suggested, but merely asked for the details of the person we were concerned about, said "thank you" and ended the call. Unbeknown to us, we would find ourselves in a similar position six years later, but next time the outcome would be far more devastating.

We continued to phone Ben's mobile number as the news deteriorated, announcing four passengers had been killed and a further seventy injured. Not knowing what to do next, we phoned RAF Cranwell and explained the situation. They said that they had been made aware of the crash and confirmed that Ben had not arrived yet, but they would let us know when he did.

We were frantic with worry but there was nothing else we could do except sit, wait and watch the television in the hope that we would see Ben amongst the survivors. Then, at 5.00pm, the telephone rang and we feared the worst. "Hi, what's up?" said the voice at the end of the phone. It was Ben. We told him about the train crash and that one of the derailed carriages was the one he had a ticket for. When he had eventually arrived at RAF Cranwell, they had informed him of the rail crash and told him his parents had phoned because they were concerned he was booked on that train and asked him to phone us. Ben said he hadn't known about the crash until he arrived at RAF Cranwell. He had missed the train at Kings Cross. Having dashed onto the platform just in time to see the train pulling out of the station, his only option was to wait for the next one. A short while later, after the crash had taken place, the public service announcement at Kings Cross station casually announced that there was a problem on the line and all trains to Leeds were being rerouted. Fearing he would be late for his interview, he rang RAF Cranwell from a phone box, told them that he'd missed the train and they told him which other train to catch. This was not his first interview at RAF Cranwell; he had been to Cranwell two or three times prior to that day and had never missed the train before. He said we were unable to contact him on his mobile phone because his battery was flat. We were just thankful that he was safe.

Ben left home to embark on his RAF career on 2 January 2001, twenty-six days before his twentieth birthday. He was looking forward to going and to eventually be able to say he was in the RAF, but at the same time, there was some sadness as he was leaving a girlfriend behind. Although he had previously passed his driving test and was the owner of an old, blue Ford Escort car, one of his close friends, and the uncle of his girlfriend, took him up to RAF Cranwell to begin his career.

Ben seemed to strive to be unpredictable, to surprise people, so much so that to his own annoyance he became predictable. Whilst training at RAF Cranwell, he would suddenly appear on our doorstep at weekends after previously saying he wouldn't be coming home that weekend. Some months later, he treated himself to a new car – a brand new silver convertible with a foldaway hardtop. He was delighted with his car and loved being able to lower or raise the roof as he was waiting in a line of traffic. At the weekends, when he had told us he would be coming home, he would phone us and ask what the weather was like down in Somerset so he could raise or lower the car roof accordingly. Often he would just arrive at our house in the early hours of Saturday morning and would be surprised when we weren't surprised to see him. Gra and I mused over the fact that he was so predictably unpredictable that, to Ben's slight annoyance, whatever he did never really surprised us – that was until the loss of Nimrod XV230.

Ben survived his training at RAF Cranwell, but in a letter he wrote to me shortly after joining, he said he did find it a bit of a culture shock initially. When he had completed his initial training, Gra and I went to his passing out day at Cranwell and stood alongside his girlfriend. Ben looked so smart in his No 1 uniform, his white gloves hanging over his belt. It was a proud day for all of us, especially when he was presented with his wings. During the flypast, Gra's emotions got the better of him and a few tears rolled down his cheeks as we watched in silence. I asked him why the tears and he said it was because he was so proud of Ben.

When he finished his training, he was told that his first posting would be to RAF Kinloss in the north of Scotland where he would be flying on Nimrods. I was pleased to see Ben progressing in his chosen career but slightly sad that he would be so far away from home. He went from living at one end of the country in sleepy Somerset to working at the other end, on the beautiful Moray Coast of the north of Scotland. I was also concerned how he and his girlfriend would manage with so many miles between them, for Ben was not going to be able to return home most weekends like he had been doing while stationed at RAF Cranwell. When Ben returned from Cranwell, which happened to be most weekends, his girlfriend would stay at our house with him and I knew it was going to be difficult for both of them being at opposite ends of the country.

While Ben was waiting for his posting to RAF Kinloss to begin, he was chosen by a production company to take part in a TV documentary. Tigress Productions were making a documentary about the Dambusters for Channel 4 and the Discovery Channel and wanted to use a young aircrew to simulate one of the Dambusters raids. They had commissioned BAFTA award winning director Gary Johnstone to make the programme, but they needed their Dambusters. They wanted eight RAF graduates to be put through their paces to see if the modern day crew could match the skill of those who flew in 1943, testing their airborne navigation, piloting and bombing skills, and ultimately get them to recreate in the studio the original Dambusters mission.

Ben was proud and excited to have been chosen. He had the opportunity to meet some of the original Dambusters crew and travel to Canada to fly in a restored Lancaster bomber, one of only two in the world left flying. The documentary was three hours long, and much of it was filmed in a sophisticated simulator designed and built by Southampton University to replicate the interior of a full size, seven crew Lancaster bomber. The young RAF crew, in their simulator, were successful in emulating the achievement of their predecessors; they hit the target, destroyed the dam and made it home. To accompany the documentary series, a book was also produced entitled simply *The Dambusters* by John Sweetman, David Coward and Gary Johnstone. When the book went on sale in the shops, I immediately bought a copy. However, that didn't stop me from going into WHSmith on occasions just so I could open the book on the shelf and see Ben looking back at me with a smile on his face. We were so proud of him.

The day eventually arrived for Ben to travel to RAF Kinloss and begin his new life, hundreds of miles away. He drove around to his girlfriend's house to say his goodbyes to her and her family, but instead of leaving her at the house, they quickly agreed between the two of them that she would travel some of the way to Scotland with him then catch a train back. We were not at all surprised for I knew it was going to be very difficult for him to leave her behind in Somerset. However, the plan for his girlfriend to travel only part way to Scotland didn't work out as they had anticipated, and she ended up travelling all the way to the north of Scotland with him – again we were not at all surprised. I believe she stayed with him for a number of weeks before she returned home to Somerset.

Ben had only been in Scotland for a week or two when they experienced heavy snowfalls. . Here in Somerset, snow is not something that is seen every year. However, in the last couple of years, Somerset has had exceptional snowfalls. Ben sent us a video taken on his mobile phone showing the heavily falling snowflakes as they quickly and quietly covered the scenery in a blanket of white. The video was taken through his bedroom window on the airbase. It's a video which we still have and is a very poignant reminder of our son.

Ben loved his job but really missed his girlfriend, so a few months after he started his career at RAF Kinloss, she moved to the north of Scotland to be with him. With the two of them now living in Scotland, it wasn't long before they began looking for accommodation outside of the airbase. They found a house in Forres, a town just a couple of miles from the airbase. The house was available to rent, so the two of them moved into it. Before long they were discussing buying a place of their own, so when Ben asked us if we could help financially, we lent him the deposit on a new bungalow on the outskirts of the town.

During his time on Nimrods, Ben went on a round-the-world trip with the aircraft. He visited Cyprus, Bahrain, Diego Garcia, Australia, Fiji, Hawaii, California,

Newfoundland, then back to Scotland. He continued his career in the RAF doing a number of tours of duty in Iraq and Afghanistan. It was after one of his tours of duty in 2005 that he rang his father up and said he was thinking of moving again. He said if the airbase closed – and there had been rumours at the time that RAF Kinloss could possibly close in the future – then his bungalow in Forres could be worth less than he had bought it for. He was also concerned that it might be difficult to sell if there was a surplus of houses on the market. He said he had seen a house in Inverness that he would like to buy but couldn't afford the deposit. As he'd paid back most of the money that we had previously lent him for the bungalow, we agreed to lend him some more so he could buy the house in Inverness. As long as we had the money available to us, I don't think we would ever have turned down such a request from any of our three children because that's what parents do – support their children. We would never have got our feet on the housing ladder had it not have been for our own parents helping us all those years ago.

Gra and I would go up to Scotland and stay with Ben and his girlfriend twice a year. We stayed with them at all the three properties they shared together. The house at Westhill overlooked the Moray Firth and the Black Isle, beyond which were the snow-capped mountains of the north of Scotland; it was a truly breath taking view, and I never got tired of looking at, although I believe the magnificent view is now sadly obstructed by further housing development.

On Thursday 13 July 2006, Andy and Gra travelled to Inverness for a long weekend with Ben at his house. Matt and his partner also went for the weekend. I was unable to go as I had to work, but I telephoned Ben and had a chat to him on the Friday afternoon. I had asked Gra to take a photograph of Andy, Matt and Ben together. Every so many years since they were born, we had taken a photo of the three of them together, but now that they were grown up and led separate lives, with Ben hundreds of miles away, there were less occasions for such photographic opportunities. However, I insisted to Gra that he must take a photograph of the three of them before he returned home, which he eventually did. We didn't know it at the time, but that photograph taken the weekend of 15–16 July 2006 was the final photograph of the three of them together. I am so glad it was taken.

Andy returned home on the Monday but enjoyed his visit so much that he returned to Ben's on the Wednesday for a further five days. The following weekend, Ben and his fiancée drove down to Somerset for a few days holiday. On Thursday 3 August 2006, Gra and I saw Ben for the very last time. I stood in the fading summer sun of our front garden, gave him a hug and told him I loved him.

He gave me one of his big bear hugs back and said, "I love you too, Mother."

Later that day, they returned to Inverness and Ben flew out to the Gulf on Saturday 19 August 2006. He was due to arrive back at RAF Kinloss on Saturday 11th November 2006.

Family holiday Canford Cliffs, aged 2

Ben aged 8, and Trish

Above: Ben aged 2, Andy
aged 8 and Matt aged 3

Right: School photo, aged 11

Ben outside The White House, Washington DC

3

The Long Wait

Monday 4 September was another dreadful day we had to face. We were finding it very, very difficult to grasp the enormity of what had happened and were totally distraught. Many kind and concerned people visited us at the house, offering their condolences, but it didn't ease the agony and desolation that lay heavy within us. It all seemed so unreal, as if we had entered a completely different world – a world detached from reality and from where we were no longer players, just static spectators of a gruesome spectacle.

Our VO informed us that the press would like to speak to any relatives who felt emotionally strong enough to face the cameras and public, however they accepted that it might be too distressing so soon after the crash.

Gra said he wanted to give a short statement to the press. He said he wanted to tell the country what a beautiful boy Ben was. Andy said he would prepare and read a short statement on behalf of the family; his job as a fraud officer meant he was more accustomed to speaking in public than the rest of the family. It was arranged that we would all travel to the airbase from where Andy would read his prepared statement to the press. I desperately wanted to go to the airbase as I felt I would be spiritually closer to Ben there, for this was where he worked and lived. Our VO said he would drive us to the airbase, a journey that took about forty minutes. The road runs parallel to the Moray Firth and the single-track railway line that links the Highlands with the rest of Scotland, and passes beside luscious green fields scattered with grazing cows. Along the roadside, tired summer flowers bowed their heads as if in a mark of respect. During the journey, our VO informed us about the abundance of floral tributes that were being laid at the main entrance of the airbase and about the many journalists awaiting the first contact with relatives.

When we arrived at the main gate of the airbase, the flowers and cards were clear for all to see, and so too were the waiting cameramen and journalists on the opposite side of the road. As the car slowed, our VO showed his security pass and we were waved through by the guard. This was not my first visit to the airbase; Ben had taken me there in his car once before to show me where he worked and spent so much of his time. That had been a happy occasion and Ben had been so proud to show me around. I never imagined then that I would be returning under such dreadful circumstances. As we approached the main building, all I could think about was Ben and how much I loved him. We drove slowly along the front of the buildings and parked outside the main entrance. I felt myself struggle for breath as the world I was in became more unrecognisable and was quietly suffocating me.

We left the safety of the vehicle and proceeded into the building. Inside were a number of military personnel waiting to greet us. They all had a sombre look on their faces and appeared slightly nervous, probably because so many relatives were expected throughout the day.

We were welcomed by a number of officers who offered their condolences and ushered us quietly through to one of the many rooms. This was the first time I had been inside one of the buildings and it struck me how very dated it appeared. The room was large and antiquated, and had a smell of bygone times, with a very authoritarian air to it. Pictures offering snippets of past years hung proudly on the walls. It was as if the room knew it was representing the Government and the Crown and possessed the solemnity demanded by such a huge responsibility. As Gra glanced at one of the pictures, an officer came up to him and quietly told him that the Nimrod in the picture he was looking at had also crashed on the 2nd of September, but eleven years earlier. It had crashed into a lake whilst performing at an air show in Canada and all those on board were killed.

A woman dressed in a smart blue RAF uniform entered the room and offered her condolences. She politely explained to us that it was her job to liaise between the relatives and the media. She asked which members of the family were going to address the waiting press and did we know what we were going to say. Gra said nothing, which surprised me because earlier he had said he wanted to talk to the press. Andy, however, was as reliable as always and had prepared a short statement and printed it out. The RAF liaison officer was surprised and pleased with his preparation and asked Andy if she could photocopy the statement and provide the waiting press with copies, plus take a copy for herself. Andy agreed. She then asked where the family would like to stand for the reading of the statement. I thought we would be seated behind a desk in a room, with the press the other side of the desk. This is the layout I had seen when I had watched other press conferences on the television news channels. However, she informed us that because of security the press would not be allowed onto the airbase. She suggested to Andy that he stand on an area of grass opposite the main entrance to the airbase. The cameras would then be able to film the interview then turn around and film the many floral wreathes and messages that had been left at the main entrance. With that agreed, and copies of Andy's statement in her hand, she left the room and proceeded in the direction of the waiting press. She returned after about ten minutes, confirming that everything had been 'put in place' and that the press were ready and awaiting our arrival.

It all seemed a rather surreal situation to us. Reading a statement to the press was something you watched on the television, being done by other people. But here we were, in a state of disbelief and shock, about to do it ourselves. The RAF and the media were telling me Ben was dead, and that I needed to do this, this and this – so I was doing it. But I don't think I really believed Ben was dead. I felt I was in a kind of limbo; the authorities were saying he was dead and I was answering yes, but at the same time thinking no. Well, how could he be? He was only twenty-five and he was my Ben. People are supposed to die in order of age. You don't die until you are at least in your seventies, you certainly don't die at twenty-five. That was just not fair, not acceptable.

We left the large antiquated room with its smell of bygone times and emerged into the glare of the September sunshine. We headed back to the vehicles which we had arrived in only a short time earlier. Our VO drove Andy, Matt and Gra back to the main gate and across the road to where the press were waiting. I followed behind in one of the other cars. We kept quite a distance behind, as we did not want the press connecting the two cars and hence taking photographs of us. The plan seemed to work well, and Andy, Matt and Gra took their allotted position on the neat lawn opposite the entrance to the airbase. The RAF liaison officer announced to the waiting press that Andy would read a short statement but wouldn't answer any questions.

When instructed by her, Andy began to read his prepared statement:

On behalf of my family and Ben's fiancée and everyone who knew him, I just want to say a few words about my little brother. Sergeant Ben Knight, or Tapper as he was known to his friends, was a loving son, brother, fiancée, uncle, nephew, cousin and friend. Everything Ben did, he did with dignity and bravery and with an energy for life that touched everyone he met. He represented vitality and strength and freedom. He loved flying, and he died doing what he loved and what he believed in to ensure that the people of Afghanistan can enjoy the same freedom that he did. Our thoughts and prayers are with the other families and friends of Ben's fellow crew members. As a family, we wish to extend our heartfelt thanks to the members of staff at the RAF who have helped us through this and supported us through this difficult time.

Matt cried all the way through the reading, a low, heartbreaking cry that appeared to come from deep within him. Andy reached out to him with a comforting hand in an attempt to stem his tears, but to no avail – his pain was too deep. Gra wept quietly, his arm around Matt. I sat in the other car, reflecting on how far from reality I had felt since being told of Ben's death on Saturday, and I was unsure whether I would ever find my way back.

When Andy had finished reading his statement, Gra suddenly decided he wanted to say a few words. He had not prepared anything in writing but stepped nearer to the microphone and with tears in his eyes simply added:

I hate flying. I didn't want him to be in planes but that is what he wanted to do. He was flying with the birds, now he is flying with the angels, and God is with him.

Gra and I did not know exactly what Andy had written in his statement but he was very articulate so we knew it would be compassionate and appropriate. We can never thank Andy enough for the words he spoke that very sad Monday morning outside RAF Kinloss.

When Andy and Gra had finished speaking, the press wanted to ask them questions but the RAF liaison officer could see that Andy, Matt and Gra were not up to that and ushered the press away. Andy, Matt and Gra then climbed into the car and we were all driven back across the road and into the airbase again. When we were all safely back inside the building, the RAF liaison officer congratulated them again, saying how well they did.

A successful operation – and we were to experience many more so-called 'operations' as the days, weeks and months went by.

In the afternoon, our VOs drove us back to the house in Inverness. When we arrived at the house, more people had congregated to offer their condolences. Some were relatives, some friends and others RAF officials. So many people! It was such a bewildering time – so very difficult to take in the enormity of what we were being told.

Throughout the rest of that day, and indeed the following days and weeks, many people came, offered their condolences then left. Some stayed longer than others, but all were full of disbelief that such a terrible accident could have occurred. We were introduced to many people in the first few weeks following the loss of XV230. Some were friends and work colleagues of Ben, others held far senior posts to Ben and knew him on a purely professional level. All of them were very kind and deeply upset by the tragic deaths of the fourteen men on board the aircraft... but it didn't bring Ben back. My Ben was still dead and would always be dead from now on. He was twenty-five and loved life. He should not have been dead. I loved him so much.

It was the day after the press interview, Tuesday 5 September 2006, and nearly every daily national newspaper carried large two or three page articles about yesterday's statement by Andy, Matt and Gra. I remembered a line from one of Ben's favourite films, *Top Gun* – "How's it feel to be on the front page of every newspaper in the English speaking world?" But we were not in a film. This was real life, and it felt awful. Inside the newspapers were many articles about Ben and his colleagues. Matt was pictured with his hand over his face, crying, and Gra was shown ashen-faced and weary, while Andy was praised for his statement and composure as he spoke to the press and media. My favourite RAF photograph of Ben had been minimised, relegated to black and white, and now appeared in nearly every daily newspaper. Again, the papers were saying Ben was dead. Every newspaper said he and the rest of the crew, known as Crew 3, were dead, along with two additional men, one from the Parachute Regiment and one from the Royal Marines. The newspaper articles and television coverage labelled them all as 'heroes'. But I didn't want a dead hero; I just wanted Ben, my youngest child. I could not comprehend that I would never, ever see him again. The situation didn't seem real and I found it all so very difficult and confusing. For the newspapers and television it was just another story and their coverage was widespread, making it feel even more unreal. I felt if I could just step back from the media coverage, step out of the news items, then maybe I could find my way back to my life before 2 September 2006, where everything was ordinary and normal and I had three children – Andy, Matt and Ben. Looking back, I can see that I didn't realise how important the media would become to us over the months and years to come.

It was only four days since the crash of Ben's aircraft, but we had already received many letters praising those on board. Some of the letters were from high-ranking RAF personnel, others were from families that had also lost loved ones within the RAF. People were being so kind, but it didn't alter the end result; Ben was still dead. The television news channels were showing Andy reading his statement again and again, praising his delivery. But I just wanted Ben back. Sometimes I felt a little foolish, for I think many outsiders would probably have said that he was in a dangerous occupation and that these tragedies happen in such circumstances. Indeed, I would have been one to say that before Ben joined the RAF. Each time he was preparing to fly off to Iraq or some other danger zone, I would always say to him, "Be careful, I love you." He would always reply, "I know, Mother, I love you too. We are three miles up, no one can get us." I believed him and took comfort from what he said, that no one could reach them that high above the earth. I found myself feeling very cross with him for dying. I wanted to say to him, "You told me you were safe up there and I believed you." How could he have got it so wrong? I was really very cross with him in the beginning. I wanted him stood in front of me so I could question him and tell him off for getting killed, but as the months passed and more information came to light, I realised that he had indeed believed he was safe.

The rest of that harrowing first week seemed to pass so quickly. On one of the days that week, we drove over to the airbase to lay some flowers and tributes to Ben at the main gate. We were also invited onto the base to talk with senior officers and were given the opportunity to look inside one of the other Nimrod aircraft. I accepted their offer, as I wanted to see where Ben would have been sat on the aircraft on the day of the crash. Gra, however, could not bear to step inside the Nimrod; he said it was too painful for him to see where Ben would have been sitting.

All through that first week, RAF people came and went, so did Ben's friends and work colleagues. The house was full with family from both sides. We continued to receive many official letters and cards: one from the MOD; another from Royal Air Force Headquarters Strike Command; one from Royal Air Force Headquarters No 2 Group; one from Royal Air Force Chief of Air Staff; another from RAF Kinloss; some from people who had experienced a similar horror to the one we were now going through; and others from people that just wanted to say how very sorry they were for us. We even got one from the Prime Minister, Tony Blair. I have kept them all. As you would expect, they all offered their condolences and sent offers of help, but there wasn't really anything any of them could do. If they could not bring Ben back to life, then there was nothing they could do to help.

On the first Thursday after the crash, we were informed that all the bodies had been recovered. However, I was shortly to discover the true meaning and the horrific reality of that statement. In the beginning, I didn't understand why it would take days as opposed to hours to confirm the bodies had been found. But as the days passed and reality of the crash emerged, the full horror of the circumstances gradually became apparent to me.

The following day, Friday 8 September, we were told that the crew would be returned to Kinloss on Tuesday 12 September. Usually, within the Armed Forces, the bodies of those who have been killed abroad have to be returned to RAF Lyneham in Wiltshire and the families would be expected to travel there for the Repatriation Ceremony. However, this was an exceptional situation. It was the largest loss of British military life in a single incident since the Falklands War, and permission had been obtained from the Ministry of Defence to return the crew of Nimrod XV230 to their home base at RAF Kinloss. On hearing that, I thought "what good news", but classing it as such just served to remind me of how far away from ordinary life and reality I had become.

The day we heard that information was also Matt's birthday.

I had insisted the day before that I must go to a shop and buy him a birthday card. Although this was the worst week of my life, it was still his birthday and I felt it should be acknowledged. I didn't want Matt to feel forgotten or ignored. He had flown back home the previous day as his partner, later to become his wife, was six months pregnant with their first child. He returned the following Monday in time for the Repatriation Ceremony on the Tuesday.

At the weekend, I went into Inverness with Andy to look for a suitable coat to wear to the Repatriation Ceremony. When we travelled up to Scotland a week ago, I had not thought to pack a coat. We had hurriedly thrown some clothes into a suitcase on that fateful Saturday evening, but we were totally oblivious as to what lay ahead of us and what attire would be required. However, to be shopping at such a dreadful time seemed incongruous and irreverent, but it was something that had to be done for I needed appropriate and warm clothing. It was far from a usual shopping trip and many times I had to shake myself to remind me of the circumstances under which I was there. Andy was very helpful, though, and I soon chose a plain black coat.

Andy, Matt and Ben all look very similar, and a few of Ben's colleagues asked if Andy was Ben's twin. Often, when Andy and Matt were talking together, I could see Ben in their facial expressions. At the time of Ben's death, Andy had more time available to him than Matt did, and so spent more time at Ben's house than Matt. As the house was new, Ben had not finished landscaping the back garden and had really only just begun. In the days and weeks following Ben's death, Andy and a colleague of Ben's spent a lot of their time digging in the garden. Andy had been made aware of Ben's intended plans for the garden, so between them they set about digging a fish pond, laying pavements, putting down turf and planting shrubs until the garden was completed. It also gave them something else to think about, apart from the awful situation we all found ourselves in. Sometimes I would glance out of the window, and for a split second, I would see Ben digging, not Andy.

One of the many visitors to the house at that time was Deborah; she was a good friend of Ben's, and she usually popped in everyday to see how we were all doing and ask if we needed anything. Over the months, Deborah and Andy became close friends and eventually became a couple. About a year later, Deborah moved to Somerset, and she and Andy returned to the Scottish Highlands in December 2008 to get married. They now have two gorgeous children, twins Poppy and Thomas. It is strange to think that such a loving and happy relationship only developed due to Ben's sudden and tragic death.

We continued to stay at the house in Inverness until the beginning of December and we soon descended into a disorganized routine. Gra was usually the first one to wake in the morning and would dress in the dark so as not to disturb me. He would then creep downstairs, make himself a cup of tea, and carry it through the utility room and into the garage. It was here that he spent a lot of his time, sometimes crying, sometimes thinking and sometimes smoking.

Ben and his fiancée had only moved into the house eight months earlier, in January of 2006. We first went to stay with them at their new home about six weeks after they had moved in. The day we arrived they were both at work, but Ben had told us where to find the door key. When we had let ourselves into the house there was a note waiting for us on the table, written in Ben's untidy handwriting. To me, his handwriting looked as though it had been written by a spider crawling across the page. It read: Dad, if you want a fag, go in the garage. Love, Ben. It made us smile and we kept the note. We still have it to this day. Strange how even a scrap of paper with a hurriedly written note on it takes on a new importance.

Every time Gra entered the garage, he was reminded of Ben and his note. But Ben would never see his garage again; he would never open the door and say to Gra, "You in here again, Father? Those things are going to kill you", and then shut the door as quickly as he had opened it so as to not let the smoke travel through the utility room and into the house. It was very hard for Gra to sit in that garage day after day, but the alternative was to stand outside and allow the bitter cold of the north wind to bite at his skin, something he was not used to in Somerset. So it had to be the garage. He would sit on one of the yet-to-be-unpacked boxes next to Ben's car and smoke his cigarette. However, there were so many painful reminders in that garage that he usually ended up in tears. As he sat there in silence, the unpacked boxes and the car his only company, memories of happier times shared with Ben would flash across his thoughts forcing even more tears from his red eyes. The car was a Silver Ford Cougar, which Gra and Ben had bought together shortly before Ben moved to RAF Kinloss. When Gra had told me what car Ben had bought, I was not surprised; that car was very much *Ben*. Ben told his father, some months later, that he never expected him to agree to the purchase of such a sleek and fast car. However, as *Top Gun* had been one of Ben's favourite films and Cougar one of the main characters, Gra knew once Ben had seen the car that there was no other one for him. Ben loved his car, but now it sat quiet and dejected alone in the garage, like a faithful dog waiting for his master to come home not realising his master would never return home again.

Gra had trained as a psychiatric nurse so he was familiar with grief counselling and the book *The Five Stages of Grief* by Elisabeth Kübler-Ross, but now he had become the patient/client and the situation was reversed; all that he had learnt took on a different meaning. He tried so hard to provide us with some sort of normality in those early days after Ben's death, but normality had become so distorted we were floundering in our grief.

As the days turned into weeks, I was at a loss as to how I was going to cope with this dreadful situation I had been thrust into. How could I cope with the death of my child?

In an attempt to try and understand, and in order for me to keep functioning, I decided to buy a copy of the book *Goodbye, Dearest Holly* by Kevin Wells. His daughter was killed in Soham in the summer of 2002. I had considered purchasing the book when it was first published, but the horror of losing a child was too much for me to confront at a time when I didn't need to confront it. However, now that I was faced with that situation, I desperately needed to know how to cope and whether I could survive this horror. I also purchased a copy of *Sara Payne: A Mother's Story* – again, I felt I was desperate for a way of coping. I am not usually a fast reader but I devoured those two books quicker than I had ever read anything before. While I was reading them, I felt I was not so alone; I was in the company of someone else who knew what it was like to suddenly be informed that their child had been killed and find themselves in the glare of the media. I hope this book will help other people as those two books helped me. I suppose I should have considered obtaining some help from the counselling services, but I was away from home and none was ever offered by the RAF. I was certainly not in any fit state in those early days and weeks to go in search of it myself.

On one of the daily visits to the house, our VO informed us of an internet site called PPRuNe: Professional Pilots Rumour Network, which contained a military section where RAF personnel had started a 'Nimrod Condolences' thread. There were many tributes on there to Ben and the rest of the crew, and their kind words were greatly appreciated.

As the weeks turned into months and the months turned into years, PPRuNe became a part of our lives. Many people shared information with Gra regarding the airworthiness of XV230 via the site, and some of those people have remained very loyal to our cause of identifying who was responsible for killing Ben and why it was allowed to happen. We will always be truly grateful for their help and friendship.

There have been times when some people on PPRuNe, and a similar website E-Goat, have criticized our determination to expose the truth about airworthiness within the RAF, and at times I have found such criticism very upsetting. Two people in particular, who were unidentifiable to us as they both used pseudonyms, were extremely hurtful. One wrongly implied we had been awarded a six-figure sum by the Courts in respect of Ben's death, and insisted on making very nasty comments about us. On another occasion, someone anonymously accused us of suing Ben's fiancée 'for half of her war pension and the house'. I don't know why these people made such defamatory remarks, which were totally unfounded, but I think Ben would have been absolutely disgusted by their behaviour. We also received an email from someone accusing us of embarking on vindictive and malicious litigation against Ben's fiancée, when we did no such thing. In reality, it was Ben's fiancée that took litigation against me in the Scottish Courts in early 2007 – a fact that I should imagine can be easily checked against the Inverness Court records. It is my view that such accusations could not have come from anyone close to Ben or anyone that truly cared for him. I found the comments aimed mainly at Gra to be particularly upsetting. Gra has always been very strong about such hurtful comments, although I know he too has found them distressing. But he has always said his only concern has been to find out why Ben's aircraft crashed and who was responsible. However, I have never been able to understand how some people can make such cruel comments at a time when we were grieving so painfully for our youngest child, and for that I can never forgive them.

When *The Nimrod Review* by Charles Haddon-Cave QC was published on 28 October 2009, it gave a damning report surrounding the loss of Nimrod XV230 and a great many people realised then that our concerns with safety were justified. The following paragraph is taken from the *Review*:

> *My report concludes that the accident to XV230 was avoidable, and that XV230 was lost because of a systemic breach of the Military Covenant brought about by significant failures on the part of the MOD, BAE Systems and QinetiQ. This must not be allowed to happen again.*

4

Ben Comes Home – The Repatriation Ceremony

Tuesday 13 September 2006 was the day Ben was brought home, dead. By midday, he was safely back on home soil. It was good to have him back.

I attended a meeting at RAF Kinloss the previous evening at which the families had the itinerary for the Repatriation Ceremony presented to them. It was read out in a military manner by an RAF Officer who concluded, "16.30 hours, operation complete". At the time, Gra and I were aghast that such a situation as this was being presented to us as a military operation, but over the months and years we became accustomed to the military ways and terms. Although, I still feel the manner in which that meeting was held was certainly not appropriate.

That Tuesday morning was the first morning since the crash that we were all awake and out of our beds early. We all had to be at the airbase for 9.30am and it had been agreed that we would travel in our VO's car. A coach had been arranged to transport the rest of our relatives to the Repatriation.

As duly instructed, we arrived at the airbase at about 9.20am. It had previously been arranged that all 'guests' attending the Repatriation Ceremony would enter the airbase at Crash Gate 3. This was so we could avoid any press and photographers that may have been waiting at the main gate hoping to take pictures of the relatives. It seemed strange to me at the time that so much interest could surround so much grief, and the more serious the event, the greater the public interest. They hovered like hawks, waiting for that one special photograph or phrase that would make money for them around the world. I can't recall any occasions in those early days when the media irritated or upset me by their presence. I knew they were usually there, lurking somewhere in the background, but my grief had taken a grip of me and shielded me from the daily reality of the outside world. After all, they were just doing their job, just doing what they had to do.

Once inside the airbase, we were ushered into one of the many antiquated rooms where tea and coffee were being served to one side. Although we arrived on time, some guests were already there and the room soon filled up as even more relatives, VIPs and RAF personnel arrived. We talked quietly amongst ourselves, still trying to take in the enormity of what had happened. At 10.30am, the Duke of Edinburgh arrived. He slowly moved around the room, accompanied by his staff, and was introduced to most of the relatives. Obviously, we didn't have anything in common with him; however, he did appear to have the ability to make polite conversation without upsetting anyone. On reflection, it must have been difficult for him as he endeavoured to sound compassionate and caring in a situation where words, however well meant, are utterly inadequate.

At 11.15, we all boarded the coach that was to take us to the designated area on the runway that had been prepared for the Repatriation – and ultimately to Ben. There were four coaches in total, and when everyone was aboard, the coaches began their sad journey, travelling slowly through the airbase and out to the runway. Passing the many RAF buildings, I remembered how this was Ben's 'home'; he was proud and happy to walk around these buildings. He'd worked hard to get here and now he was dead.

Before we arrived at the area that had been cordoned

off for the Repatriation Ceremony, we passed a section that was reserved for RAF personnel. A great many of them had already gathered there, dressed in their smart blue uniforms, awaiting the return of the ill-fated crew. As we passed slowly by, they gazed at the procession of coaches with their sad cargo. Gra and I gazed back at them, wishing that we could have been like them, on the outside looking in instead of the other way round. Seeing them all standing there in the early autumn sunshine beneath a brilliant blue sky was torture for me. I thought that Ben should be standing there, tall and proud in his uniform, not dead in a wooden box.

Out of a window on the opposite side of the coach, I caught a glimpse of a fleet of hearses lined up in readiness. I turned away quickly, not wanting to believe what I had just seen. As we continued further along the runway, we passed the press area. A temporary platform made from scaffolding had been hastily erected for them and was covered with media people, cameras and microphones. The BBC covered the entire event live on their news channel. Although they had all written sensitively and caringly about the crew and explosion of XV230 since the incident happened, for some reason today they really did seem like birds of prey to me – all perched high on their branch of scaffolding waiting to swoop.

The coaches continued slowly on their momentous journey and eventually came to a stop outside a large open fronted marquee. When instructed to, we all disembarked from the coaches and slowly and quietly took our places amongst the perfectly aligned chairs, with spouse and next of kin being ushered to the front rows. Andy sat in the front row of chairs with Ben's fiancée. Gra and I were seated behind, with Matt and his partner behind us. Other family members were ushered to seats further back. When all the families were seated, there seemed to be a long wait until the arrival of the Duke of Edinburgh and the other dignitaries.

When they did eventually arrive, they were seated at the front of the marquee in the centre seats. So this was it; Ben was coming home. The aircraft carrying him had left Afghanistan the previous day, following a sunset ceremony amongst their colleagues, and would soon to be arriving back on home soil.

At 12.00pm, we were instructed to stand, and as we did, one minute of silence was observed across local towns and villages in respect of the fallen servicemen. The silence was broken by the roar of the jet engines as the giant transport plane carrying the bodies landed and taxied along the runway. I felt an overwhelming sense of relief as I heard the aircraft land, for it signified that at last Ben was home. It may have been a strange thought, but I was suddenly aware that Ben's flying career was almost over – cut short by something still unknown to us at that time.

As the transport plane taxied into position, I suddenly froze on the spot. This was it, Ben was home. Tears started trickling down my cheeks. My poor Ben... I loved him so much. I wondered what he would have thought of all this. He was so full of life. I just wanted to see him one more time!

The gentle sobbing that could be heard from the other relatives increased as the aircraft came into sight of the waiting families, RAF personnel and the media. The aircraft taxied to a halt in front of the marquee, and at that precise moment, I didn't know how I was going to survive the next hour. As the aircraft slowly reached its sad destination, the noise of the engines gradually subsided and the back of the aircraft was slowly lowered. An RAF band marched sombrely into place and began to play as three clergymen positioned themselves at the rear of the plane. After a few moments, the first coffin was slowly and carefully carried from the aircraft by six pallbearers to a solemn lament from the RAF band. Draped in the Union flag, the coffin was placed with great care in one of the black funeral cars.

The sight of that first coffin shocked me back into the horrific reality of the situation. The sobbing around Gra and I increased. I really didn't know whether I was going to be strong enough to see the day through to its sad conclusion, for this was not how it was meant to end, it really wasn't. It was a horrendous situation that we, as a family, found ourselves in on that tranquil, sunny September morning.

The Duke of Edinburgh and the top RAF personnel saluted each and every coffin as it was caringly removed from the aircraft, placed in the hearse and slowly driven past the stricken families who sat in the white marquee. This was repeated thirteen more times until all of its sad cargo had been safely delivered home to RAF Kinloss. There were a number of young children at the service, some were so young that they were most probably oblivious to the horrific drama that was being played out before them and the solemnity of what was unfolding. Positioned next to Gra was a woman with a small baby; Gra put out his finger and the baby grabbed it and held it tightly as babies do. Gra said afterwards that he saw the baby as a symbol of new life and of the innocence that surrounds one so young. As tears began to trickle down his face, he said the baby just smiled at him.

It took just over an hour for the aircraft to be emptied of its fourteen coffins, and in that time, many, many tears had been shed. The RAF band played throughout and the late summer sun shone continuously. Eventually, all fourteen servicemen were returned and the band fell silent as the mourners and visitors dispersed. Although it was a very difficult hour to endure, and at times seemed unbearable, I was thankful that Ben was home.

As we all got back onto the coaches and headed for our next planned destination of the day, I felt I was a very different person. The dreadful events of that day had tainted me forever and I knew that I would never be the same again.

The coaches transported us to yet another large hall where drinks and light refreshments were being served. As expected, the staff was extremely helpful and very kind in nature. The top RAF personnel from the airbase were also present and mingled tentatively with the families. The Defence Secretary had also attended the Repatriation, and he now came to speak to us for a while. Ruth was also there; she was the RAF Padre based at RAF Lyneham. It was she who came to our house on 2 September to give us the dreadful news that Ben's aircraft had crashed and that he was 'missing presumed dead'. I told her that I didn't know how I managed to get from that awful evening to here, the Repatriation Ceremony ten days later. But somehow I had. On that Saturday evening, I felt that my life had stopped and I could not see any future or even see the next hour before me, not even the next minute. Everything about me had stopped, I was still alive but somehow my life had stopped. I tried to make sense of it all by talking to Ruth, and it was then that I asked her if she would come to Ben's funeral. Of course, she said she would. Gra somehow found himself in a conversation with the Duke of Edinburgh and said afterward how nice he was.

After the official service of removing the coffins from the aircraft had finished, each coffin was taken to a large new, yet to be commissioned, IT block on the airbase substituting as a temporary Chapel of Rest. The room had been set aside so families could spend some quiet time with their loved ones. Through the course of the afternoon, immediate family visited the hall, two or three families at a time in order to keep the proceedings as private as possible. Until it was our turn, we chatted and drank tea and tried to come to terms with the enormity of the day's events. When our turn arrived, we walked the hundred metres to the hall with some trepidation, not knowing how we were going to cope with seeing Ben's coffin.

When I entered the hall, I gasped. It was such a sad sight; it literally took my breath away. Fourteen identical coffins, each one draped in the Union flag. We didn't know which coffin was Ben's as formal identification was to be made at the John Radcliffe Hospital in Oxfordshire in the forthcoming weeks. I moved slightly away from Gra and our VO, leant up against a pillar and quietly cried. It was such a dreadful situation to be in. If Ben was supposed to be in one of the coffins then I wanted to know which one. I wanted to be able to go up to his coffin and tell him off for getting killed. I wanted to tell him to stop this nightmare and be alive again. The RAF was telling us Ben was in one of those coffins, but I couldn't see him. They said he was there – but how could I be sure if I couldn't see him? I felt I needed to see him before I believed this dreadful information people were telling me.

We stayed in that hall for about fifteen to twenty minutes just looking at all the coffins. It was the saddest sight that I have ever seen. No one should have to see what we saw that day.

The events of those ten days led me to seriously consider any belief I had in God. I was brought up to believe that God was good, but how could he be good if he let such horrific things happen to innocent people? If he truly exists and has the powers we are told he has, then why allow such horrors to happen? A good person would not be a part of such horrors; a good person would stop them happening if he had it within his power to do so.

As I stood alone in that hall, surrounded by people, I felt spiritually closer to Ben, and indeed it was the closest I had been to him since hearing of his death. I wanted so much to be able to see him; after all, he was mine. He was my 'Benny'. He only every allowed Gra and me to call him by that name and only out of ears reach of anyone other than immediate family.

Eventually, feeling drained of all strength and totally broken, we walked slowly away from the intense sadness of that coffin-filled hall, out into the emptiness of what was to be our lives from now on. As that sombre day drew to a close, our VOs drove us back to the house in Inverness. It was all such a dreadful experience that at times I found it hard to acknowledge that I was a part of it. In the evening, all the television news channels led with a lengthy report about the Repatriation Ceremony. As I looked at the pictures, I had to remind myself that I was there. At the time, it seemed peculiar and improper that something so awful for one family is just a news story to another, but I was still very unaccustomed to the way the media machine worked. For it was not until 28 January 2007, Ben's birthday, that I felt able to face my first television interview.

It had been a very upsetting day and I was glad it was drawing to a close. As always, throughout this living nightmare, I didn't know how I got from 2 September 2006 to the Repatriation Ceremony on 13 September – but somehow I did.

The following day the newspapers carried pictures and extensive stories about the previous day's Repatriation Ceremony. Most of the pictures were in colour, with some papers pointing out what they perceived to be Ben's coffin. However, until the body parts had been taken to the John Radcliffe Hospital in Oxford for the identification process to begin, true identification could not be established. Again the newspapers and the television news were saying Ben was dead, yet despite the previous day's events, I still struggled with such incongruous wording of 'Ben is dead'. Everyone I met and every situation I found myself in at that time just served to reiterate that Ben was indeed dead, but

I still struggled terribly with accepting that knowledge. To think that I would never, ever see Ben again was unbearably painful and something I struggled to understand.

5

Saying Goodbye to Ben – The Funeral

At the John Radcliffe Hospital in Oxfordshire, a team of forty-one personnel were present during the autopsies, where over four hundred separate human remains were identified by means of DNA and odontology. This took longer than we had expected and Ben's remains were not released until the beginning of November.

While we were waiting for the John Radcliffe Hospital to complete their work, our thoughts turned towards the funeral and what type of service we would all prefer. Our VO had conveyed to us that the RAF would pay for a military funeral if that is what we wanted and he had explained the amount of military involvement attached to such a funeral. We were informed that for a military funeral we would be provided with one hearse and one car for family. Limited accommodation would also available. The Union flag would be draped over the coffin and on top of the flag would lay Ben's cap, gloves and medals. These would be formally handed back to the chosen person following the funeral service. The coffin would be provided with a guard of honour as it arrived and entered the Church or Crematorium, and an RAF bearer party would carry the coffin into the service. The actual service had to include certain elements but not all were compulsory. At the end of the service, they would fold the Union flag and present it to a dedicated person, along with the cap, gloves and medals placed neatly on top. We could also have a salute given by a firing party, usually comprising of six rifleman firing three blank rounds each. To conclude the service, a fly-by from a Nimrod aircraft could also be provided.

After listening to our VO gently relay the information to us, there was a pause before I replied, "Do not expect me to be grateful that the RAF will pay for Ben's funeral. They killed him."

Our VO looked slightly uncomfortable at my response, but I certainly didn't think I had anything to thank the RAF for.

Having to arrange your own child's funeral is something no parent should ever have to do. It's the most horrendous of experiences, but of course it had to be done. Ben had often said to me that he didn't believe in God, but to the exact extent that he believed his own words, I'm not sure. I was brought up in the Roman Catholic faith and Gra in the Methodist faith, but we had not taken our children to Church on a Sunday morning since Ben was a toddler; however, the thought of having a funeral service devoid of any religious element didn't seem proper. After all, Ben had been christened when he first entered this life, and it just felt morally right that his life should conclude with a Christian service of some kind.

Together with Ben's fiancée, however, we did look into the option of a Humanist funeral service and even arranged to meet with a man who carried out such services. He came to the house in Inverness and told us a little about himself before he explained the type of service he carried out. Considering he was coming to visit a recently bereaved family, Gra and I felt he was inappropriately dressed and appeared far too casual in his manner. As soon as Gra set on eyes on him, he said he knew that this was not the type of person he wanted to conduct Ben's funeral. I agreed wholeheartedly with him. We were still in touch with Ruth, the Padre who had come to our house on 2 September to tell us Ben had been killed, and Gra and I both agreed she would be our ideal person to conduct the funeral service. She was young, down to earth and nice-looking, and we both thought Ben would have liked her. However, we wanted to respect Ben's fiancée's wishes regarding the funeral service and she was still undecided. As we had now been in the north of Scotland for about a month, Gra and I both had matters to catch up on at home so we agreed to return to Somerset for a week, allowing Ben's fiancée time to think and come to a decision about the funeral. Together with Andy and Matt, we felt a funeral service at Inverness Crematorium, conducted by Ruth, looked the best option.

When we returned to Scotland a week later, Ben's fiancée had also agreed on a service at Inverness Crematorium conducted by the RAF Padre. We agreed that if the service was going to involve the military, it would contain a certain amount of formality, and therefore to have a non-religious service seemed incongruous. As a partly religious service had already taken place at Kandahar after the bodies were recovered and again at the Repatriation, I felt that both fitted in well with what we eventually decided.

Now we had all agreed on the type and location of the service and who would conduct it, we could begin the procedure of planning the finer details of it. Because a funeral has to be planned and arrangements discussed in great length and detail, I found I had to stop on occasions and remind myself this was Ben's funeral we were planning, not some party. The turmoil within my head was because a funeral has all the hallmarks of a party – date, time, location, refreshments, accommodation, travel – and all have to be carefully planned and co-ordinated. The only difference is that everyone at a party is happy, whereas everyone at a funeral is heartbroken.

First, we all needed to decide whether we wanted any involvement from the RAF. I think we all agreed immediately that, due to the circumstances, a military funeral seemed the most appropriate; however, we excluded the firing party because to us it felt slightly alien to the RAF way of life. Gra said he didn't want a fly-by of a Nimrod aircraft at the end of the service, as it was a Nimrod that had killed Ben. However, he was overruled on that decision by myself and Ben's fiancée. Gra then added that he hoped it would snow on the day of the funeral so the heavily laden snow clouds would obscure the aircraft. Others said they wanted a clear blue sky for the day of the funeral, but in fact on the day the skies were covered with snow clouds and it did indeed snow very heavily.

Ruth was very helpful and emailed us an 'order of service' example, indicating where we could insert hymns or music. After much discussion and a few days later, we had all come to an agreement on the structure of the service. Gra printed it out so those involved in the decision-making and those attending on the day would each have a copy. The front page read *'Farewell Service for Sergeant Benjamin James Knight (Tapper)'*, with a colour picture of Ben sitting cross-legged in his flight suit and wearing his aviator sunglasses on a runway, most likely taken when he was the other side of the world. On one of his visits back home in Somerset, Ben had told me how much he liked that particular photograph, and I could never have imagined that it would shortly be fronting his funeral farewell service. I am not keen on the title 'farewell service'; it's a funeral and calling it by another name just serves to irritate me. It's a funeral and it's bloody awful, so let's just accept it for what it is and not try to disguise it into something more pleasant. Underneath the photograph was *'Inverness Crematorium Friday 17th November 2006'*. It was all so very, very upsetting seeing his favourite photograph proclaiming his funeral.

It was decided to include a picture of Ben and his fiancée on the first page of the service sheet. Ben was wearing his smart blue RAF uniform, and I understand the photograph was taken at a formal dinner they had attended. The other pages gave the order of service, which consisted of a few prayers and songs interspersed with eulogies from Ben's closest friends and school friends.

We decided to choose songs as opposed to hymns as Ben was not a churchgoer, and therefore hymns didn't seem appropriate. However, to begin the service, the RAF bearer party would enter the crematorium to the music of Elgar's *Nimrod*. As Gra and I were both of the opinion that Ben had done just what he wanted to do for most of his life and given the opportunity would have changed very little of it, our first song choice was *I've Had The Time Of My Life* by Jennifer Warnes. The second song choice was *Love of My Life* by Queen. Gra was adamant that this song should be included as he and Ben had both been keen listeners of Queen's music, and that particular song summed up Gra's feelings of loss. The next song was chosen by Ben's fiancée and was *You're Still the One* by Shania Twain. The fourth and final song was the much-chosen funeral song *Goodbye, My Lover* by James Blunt. Ben had been fond of his music and he'd had his CD playing in his car on a number of occasions when he had picked us up from Forres Station. The reason that particular track was chosen is self-explanatory.

Three of Ben's closest friends from school were asked if they would speak about the times they shared with him, as were two friends from his squash days at East Bridgwater Community Centre/Sydenham Squash Club, and also a friend from the RAF. In between the songs and the eulogies, Ruth would say the obligatory prayers and readings that would constitute a religious ceremony, thus enabling her to conduct the funeral service for Ben.

We had already paid a visit to the funeral directors in Forres and met with the owner of the company who seemed a very affable type of gentleman. I realised he was someone who was prepared to give me an honest answer, for I needed to know from him just how much of Ben there was in the coffin and in what condition. But I'm almost sure that he was hoping I would have changed my mind by the time the coffin was eventually returned to Forres. I knew such a question and its reply would require great strength and fortitude on my part but it was something I had to know. I didn't feel I had a choice. Ben was my child, I was his mother, and to me no further explanation was needed. I knew I had to ask the question and I had to have an answer. If I didn't ask, I knew I would always regret it for the rest of my life. But loitering with intent at the back of my mind was the cliché Ben so often used: *Can you handle the truth?* And I really didn't know whether I could, but within the next four weeks I would find out.

Gra and I had made plans to return home to Somerset for a long weekend when we were suddenly informed by our VO that Ben was due to be returned to the north of Scotland that weekend. He would be arriving back at Forres at 5.45pm on Saturday 4 November 2006. As we had routine tasks in Somerset that had to be addressed, we didn't cancel our journey back home. We felt it would give Ben's fiancée time alone with Ben, and as we travelled home, we received a telephone call from her to say Ben had been returned home. There were many intimate conversations shared between Ben's fiancée and myself during those difficult times, but I have not included them as they remain very personal and private and I feel they should remain so. Revisiting these events all these years later is still upsetting for me.

Ben's fiancée had said to us a few weeks earlier that she and Ben were going to buy matching wedding rings once they had decided on a date to get married. She said she still wanted to buy the rings and put Ben's in his coffin. However, we told her that, as Ben was going to be cremated, the ring would have to be removed before the cremation could take place. Once the rings were bought, the undertaker allowed her to drop Ben's ring into the corner of the coffin but said it could only remain there for a limited time as the coffin needed to be sealed, I think mainly due to the smell of decomposing flesh. Twelve months later, someone released the above information to one of the Sunday newspapers without our knowledge.

After a few days in Somerset, catching up with necessities and well-wishers, Gra and I arrived back in Scotland. With the funeral looming, there was much to be arranged. Before a cremation can take place, forms have to be completed, so one afternoon our VO came to the house with the relevant paperwork. I felt some of the questions asked on the forms didn't seem appropriate to our particular situation, but then I was thinking about every question literally. One question asked for the place of death – meaning nursing home, hospital name, house, etc. – but we understood Ben had been killed in the sky about 3,000 feet up, so initially we were not quite sure what to write down. Likewise, another question asked the time of death and again we were unsure how to answer; it is believed the aircraft exploded at about 4.30pm local time which equates to about 12.30pm our time, but which of the times should we write down? Another question asked, "Was anyone present at the time of death?" Again, I didn't know how we should answer, as there were thirteen other crew members with Ben when they were all killed.

And so the questions continued. With the help of our VO, we eventually managed to answer all the questions on the form to the best of our ability, only to move on to the next form. The second form was an RAF pro forma regarding the funeral arrangements and the amount of military involvement. Some of the questions asked included: are swords to be used at the funeral service? Is a gun salute required? Are we having a flypast? And if so, what would be the grid reference for the aircraft? Again, the seemingly unusual and unanswerable questions continued. Our VO was very helpful, as always, and eventually we managed to get all the forms completed.

In the evening, Gra and I agreed we needed a change of scenery and decided to go for a ride out in the car. We turned on the car radio only to be confronted with a programme discussing whether there was a God, and if so, why did he let such awful things happen? If there is a God I would like to ask him that same question, but I doubt I would get a straight answer! We sat in the car listening to the programme until it finished, then drove to the twenty-four hour Tesco supermarket. At the checkout, the young male assistant asked me one of their obligatory questions: 'Have you had a nice day?' I shook my head gently in disbelief but kept my feelings hidden. I wanted to reply truthfully and say "No, I have been planning my twenty-five-year-old son's funeral", but I didn't. It wouldn't have had much meaning to him; he was only doing his job. However, at the time I did feel very strongly that staff should not be told to ask such banal questions if they are not trained to cope with the wide range of replies available to the customer.

On the afternoon of the 10th of November, we arranged to meet at the funeral directors in Forres with our VO and the RAF man who was in charge of the RAF pallbearers. There was also paperwork that needed signing by the next of kin, which officially were Gra and I. Although Ben lived with his fiancée, the laws in Scotland differ in some ways to those in England and Wales, and because Ben was not married, as his parents we were his next of kin. It also meant that Ben's 'estate' would automatically be divided between myself, Gra and our other two sons – a fact that we didn't become fully aware of until the beginning of December 2006 when we all received a letter from the solicitor.

As we travelled to the funeral directors in Forres in a car Gra had rented, Ben's fiancée told us that there had been a 'mix up' of body parts, resulting in a part being put in the wrong coffin. When the mix up had been identified, the body part was returned to the John Radcliffe Hospital in Oxfordshire for further DNA testing, which confirmed it had indeed been originally placed in the wrong coffin. We were told that the mix up had since been rectified, but it cast some doubt on whether all the other body parts had been accurately identified and returned to the correct next of kin. The three of us discussed the implications of the mix up and what bearing, if any, it held for us and our situation. We considered asking if we could have Ben's body parts retested but then realised that would only ensure that Ben's parts were in the coffin and we would still not know if a part of him was in another coffin; not unless all the other families agreed to retesting, which was not a viable proposition as two of the funerals had already taken place.

By the time we arrived at the funeral directors, we were in a quandary as to what to do. As we parked the car, our VO walked across to us and got into our car. We were joined shortly by another of the VOs. We relayed our dilemma to both of them and it was agreed we would continue the conversation inside the funeral directors.

Once inside, we were directed into a little side room where Ben's coffin stood forlornly on a stand. Some flowers lay elegantly on top but their fragrance was sadly lost. At the Repatriation Ceremony, we had seen all fourteen coffins together in a room, now we were confronted with just one coffin that held the remains of our youngest child. Gra and I were both tearful. He said afterwards that what upset him the most was the smell emanating from the room. Having been a Registered Mental Nurse, it was a smell he was familiar with... the smell of decomposing flesh, made worse with the knowledge that it was the flesh of his own son. Had his remains not been kept refrigerated for the last two months since his death? The odour suggested not. Gra only stayed in the room for a short while before choosing to go outside into the car park in search of some fresh air. As the tears trickled down his face, we both struggled with the enormity of the situation. I stayed alone in the room with Ben for a little longer. I was mesmerized by the sight of his coffin, which bore his name, date of birth and age on the lid. I placed my hand on the lid and gently stroked the wood. I then ran my hand along the underside of the coffin; by doing that, I felt I was as close to Ben as I could get, for he lay on the other side of the wood that I was gently stroking. Before leaving the room, I leant over and placed my arms around the coffin and kissed the lid. It was all very, very sad and distressing.

When Gra came back inside, we all went into the office to discuss funeral arrangements and complete the necessary paperwork. However, I could not contemplate putting the final signatures on the forms while possible doubt as to identification remained as it did. Realizing that I had strong concerns about this situation, the funeral director felt a need to contact the coroner in Oxfordshire in an attempt to verify the true nature of the mix up. Because of the lateness of the day, his phone calls went mostly unanswered; of the calls that were answered, we were mainly informed that the person we were trying to contact had gone home. Eventually, he managed to contact a coroner that had knowledge of the situation regarding our concerns and was also prepared to discuss it with us. It was decided Gra would talk with the coroner, because I personally didn't feel strong enough for such a conversation at that moment in time. Therefore, Gra withdrew to another, more private, room along the corridor. When he returned, he looked visibly shaken. The coroner had told him that there was so little left of Ben that his funeral should be allowed to continue, and that if body parts were mixed up, it was in a way inconsequential, taking into account the wider picture. Gra knew then from his conversation with the coroner that Ben, in the form we knew him, was not in that coffin. That was not what Gra wanted to hear.

Since shortly after Ben's death, I had been discussing with our VO the possibility of knowing what state Ben's body was returned in. However, Gra had never wanted to know such details, and his conversation with the coroner that early evening had left him perilously close to having those details disclosed and he was very upset. In the situation I found myself in that evening, I suddenly decided I needed to know now how much of Ben there was. The funeral director agreed to show me the *list* if I was sure that was what I really wanted. I hadn't realised there would be a list, and that word alone seemed to bring me so much closer to the harshness of the reality. I will never disclose the details of that list; it would not be right out of respect for Gra, Andy, Matt or Ben's fiancée. And, perhaps most importantly, out of respect for Ben.

From the day Ben's coffin was returned to Scotland from Oxfordshire, we usually took daily turns in travelling to the funeral directors to sit with him. I found it very peaceful in the small room with Ben's coffin. Back at the house, plans were being made for his funeral, but in the room with Ben's coffin, I found I could block out the outside world and the reality it brought with it. However, reading this account five years later, I realise now that my mental state was playing games with me, for that small room with Ben's coffin in it was indeed the major part of the horrific reality.

We all agreed that the funeral should be either on a Friday or a Monday as this would provide people with more time to travel up to Inverness, particularly those people who were travelling from the Midlands and Somerset areas. The first possible date we considered was Monday 13 November, but as this was our eldest son's birthday, we didn't think it would be proper to choose that date. I didn't want Ben's funeral to be a constant reminder to Andy each year on his birthday. The day of the funeral therefore became Friday 17 November 2006. As we had already finalised the sequence of events for the actual funeral service, all that remained to be done in that respect was to print the 'order of service'. As the RAF offered to help with the printing of them, we allowed them to do so.

It was agreed that on the day of the funeral we would arrange an evening reception for family and friends. By doing so, we could offer a place to eat for those people that were unfamiliar with the area, and it would also provide us with the opportunity to thank the many people who had travelled long distances in order to attend the service. Ben's fiancée and her VO took charge of organising the evening get-together, which was to be held in the Sergeants Mess at RAF Kinloss with the catering done in-house. It had been decided that we would provide the mourners with all of Ben's favourite foods – curry and rice, chapattis, pickled eggs, pizza, ice cream and much more.

As the day of the funeral drew nearer, we were all very busy finalising arrangements and completing lists. We needed to distinguish between family and friends and remember who was who, as well as listing which people would be making their own way to the evening reception and those that needed a place reserved for them on the coach we had hired. On the Sunday before the funeral, we sat in the computer room until midnight completing the eulogy for Ruth. Then at midnight, we phoned Andy and wished him a happy birthday for Monday, before retiring to our beds. In the morning, we all continued checking the arrangements for Friday, trying to make sure we hadn't forgotten anything. I had never had the sad task of arranging a funeral before, thank goodness, so it was very unfamiliar territory for me.

In the afternoon, we went to visit Ben at the funeral directors again. Although I didn't like to dwell on the state Ben was in, at the same time it offered me a kind of comfort. If I had known Ben was lying there in the coffin, a complete body just as he would have lain in his bed, I think I would have found it even more unbearable. As it was, I could tell myself that Ben, as I knew him, wasn't in that box that they called a coffin. It was just bits of him, which if put together, still wouldn't resemble anything like my Ben.

In the evening of what was Andy's birthday, Deborah and some friends came to visit us at the house. The conversation centred on the coming funeral and everyone's disbelief that Ben was dead. Again, I cried, as I did everyday, and told them I didn't want Ben to be dead. My Ben, dead? It couldn't possibly be! No matter how hard they tried to console me, I could not stop crying; so when they left, I went straight to bed. Sleep, although in short supply, was the only way to be rid of yet another awful day.

The following day, we spent the morning completing even more paperwork, and that afternoon, Gra and I went with one of the VOs to the crematorium. We had not been to the crematorium before, and the VO needed to organise where the different people would be seated and where any press and photographers would stand. I also wanted to play the music DVD we had compiled for the service and make sure it played satisfactorily on the music system supplied at the crematorium. I stood in the large room where the service would take place in just a few days time and the tears began to build yet again. While the VO spoke to the person in charge, I concentrated on counting the number of chairs and the number of rows of chairs. If I hadn't distracted myself in that manner then I would have had to listen to the conversation that was taking place about my dead son's funeral, and I could not cope with that. So I counted, anything there was to count I counted, until the VO had finished talking and we drove back to the house.

Once we were back at the house there was plenty to be done. The beds had to be made for those people who were going to stay and details confirmed for those that were staying in hotels. Some people were flying up to Scotland and needed to be met at the airport and either taken or directed to where they would be staying for the night. Our VOs were excellent, as always, and they helped collect and ferry people around. Gra met and drove his sister to the airbase at Kinloss with her two grown up children. They were going to be staying on the base in one of the welfare houses that had been made available to us.

Later in the afternoon, Gra and Ben's fiancée drove to Forres to collect the flowers from the florists, and afterwards, we all met up at the undertakers at 4.00pm for the dressing of the coffin. The RAF Officer who was in charge of the military side of the funeral was also in charge of the dressing ceremony, and there to watch over the proceedings were myself, Gra, Ben's fiancée and our two VOs. First the Union flag was arranged very precisely over the coffin and pinned in place, and then Ben's RAF hat and gloves were carefully positioned on top of it. It didn't take long but it was a very sad and upsetting site. After we had finished there, Gra and I went off to Forres railway station to collect my brother who had travelled up from the Midlands to be at the funeral. The site of the railway station held many happy memories for us, which had now turned into sad ones. When Ben lived in Forres, we would travel up from Somerset by train and he would meet us at the station. We usually arrived a couple of minutes before he did, and we would watch as he drove hurriedly into the station car park, pull up next to us, get out of his car and greet us both with a big hug and a kiss.

So we collected my brother from the station as planned and then drove back to Ben's house in Inverness.

Inside the house, relatives and friends quietly chatted to one and other after their long journey north, clasping warm drinks between their hands as they tried instilling some warmth into their cold bones. We had also prepared sandwiches and hot snacks for the guests who may have missed out on meals whilst travelling. Some of Ben's friends, who had arrived for his funeral, had not met up since leaving school, and likewise some of the relatives had not seen each other for quite a while.

Later that evening, when all the relatives and friends had been ferried to their overnight accommodation, there was very little to do but wait for tomorrow to arrive. As I washed up in the kitchen, I stood and looked at the photograph of Ben on top of the fridge; he looked a fine young man. It was very, very difficult arranging my own child's funeral and accepting that he was dead. Every so often, I felt I was just inches away from being able to shake myself back to normality, to before 2 September, but I could never quite succeed, because from now on, this was normality.

It was Friday 17 November 2006, the day of Ben's funeral, my youngest child. I awoke at 8.00am wondering how on earth I was going get through this dreadful day. The funeral was arranged for 1.30pm at Inverness Crematorium, which was just a couple of miles from the house on the road between Inverness and Fort William. It could be seen in the distance on the other side of Inverness when looking from Ben's back garden. The weather was cold but dry, and I didn't think we would see any of the snow Gra had been hoping for. Once I had taken a shower and got dressed, there didn't seem to be much to do on that awful morning but wait – wait for Ben's funeral. I kept glancing at one of my many photographs of Ben, reminding myself that was my Ben, not what was in the coffin. In the coffin were just bits, I told myself. Ben's life ended when the plane exploded in the air. He was long gone on his way to heaven; more of him was in heaven than in that coffin.

At around 11.00am, one of the VOs came to the house to collect us and drive us to the funeral directors where we spent a little time in the Chapel of Rest beside Ben's coffin. Andy, who had not seen the coffin since it had been returned to the funeral directors, was in tears. If there was a God, then I wanted to know why I had been chosen to be part of such a horrific experience. Why me? Why not someone else? At 12.25pm, the undertaker and his colleagues carefully transferred Ben's coffin from the sanctuary of the Chapel out into the glare of reality and into the waiting hearse. Andy and I travelled in the second funeral car behind the hearse. The cortege set off slowly towards Inverness, travelling along the country roads as opposed to going on the busy Aberdeen to Inverness road. This was Ben's final journey, and he was only twenty-five-years-old. I wondered what he would be thinking if he was looking down on us now. He would probably be annoyed at how slow we were travelling. But I was still cross with him; I still wanted an explanation from him as to how he had managed to get himself killed when he always assured me that he would be safe.

Andy and I sat in complete silence in the car. No amount of words could appease that torturous journey. We arrived at the entrance gates of the crematorium shortly before 1.30pm, just as a light rain began to fall. As snow clouds gathered overhead, I had concerns as to whether the flypast would be able to take place.

Gra, his sister, Matt, his partner and Matt's cousins were in a people carrier, driven by one of the VOs, and were all waiting to join the cortege once it had entered the crematorium grounds. However, the VO had difficulty restarting the engine, and just as our driver got out of the vehicle to go and see if he could be of any assistance, their car suddenly coughed into life and they took their place in the procession. A few minutes later, we found ourselves at the entrance of the crematorium. I silently questioned whether this was really happening to me; was I about to follow Ben's coffin into that building? This was purgatory at its worst.

We got out of the cars and waited for the RAF bearer party to take the coffin out of the hearse. The intention was that Andy would stand next to Ben's fiancée, but as the coffin was removed from the hearse, he burst into tears. Gra went over to him, put his arm around him and tried to comfort him. He told him that Ben wasn't really in the coffin, just bits of his broken body, and to try and remember Ben as we knew him – loud, happy and always on the go. The bearer party walked solemnly into the crematorium, followed by close family, as Edward Elgar's *Nimrod* played quietly in the background. The sight of Ben's coffin brought some of the mourners to tears, and as it was gently placed on the stand at the front of the hall, the bearer party sombrely withdrew, leaving Ruth to begin the service.

After Ruth had welcomed everyone to the service and said a few words about Ben, three of his closest friends from school stood at the front of the congregation and recalled some of their times spent in Ben's company. The first one to talk, Mike, recalled how much Ben enjoyed all types of sport and how he loved to win. He spoke about a memorable New Year's Eve when he and Ben got in Ben's old Ford Escort Mark 2 and drove up to London to celebrate the Millennium; how they watched the fireworks over the Thames and chatted to fellow revellers before driving home through the early hours of the morning. He also recalled the many hours he and Ben would spend playing games on the computer and how Gra had taken him and Ben up to

London two years in a row, in 1994 and 1995, to a computer exhibition at Earls Court. Then the following year, Gra had taken them to Birmingham's NEC for the Motor Show. Mike had wanted Ben to sit in one of the supercars they had at the show, but Ben had declined, saying he would never have enough money to own one so there was no point in sitting in it. The friend concluded by giving an account of a time he and Ben went to the Cribbs Causeway shopping centre in Bristol to get some clothes with £120 I had given him. He went on to say that when they arrived, Ben saw a titanium squash racquet and decided he had to buy that instead of the clothes, but that his mom and dad understood his choice and gave him some more money to get the clothes he should have bought.

Another of his school friends then said a few sentences about their school days and their friendship. A young woman spoke next. She too was an old school friend of Ben's, and I know that Ben held her friendship in high esteem. Gra found it very upsetting to listen to her speak, and I could see him wiping his tears away as she recalled their times together. She told of the time they participated in the Ten Tors challenge on Dartmoor in May 1996 and how, unsurprisingly, Ben was picked as team leader; how he had encouraged them, despite appalling weather conditions, until they reached the 8th Tor on the first day; and how, on the first night, there was a snow blizzard, and the following day, all the participants had to be taken off the moor – the first time in its history the Ten Tors challenge had ever had to be stopped. She then recalled how when she moved away to go to university, Ben would suddenly turn up and attend lectures with her and they would share boozy nights out. As she concluded her eloquent reminiscing, I wondered what Ben would have thought of all this. I hoped he would have been proud of how we'd conducted ourselves since 2 September 2006 and that he would have been in agreement with everything we'd arranged.

A piece of music followed. We had decided against hymns as Ben was not a religious person, and to have surrounded him by such didn't seem a correct nor compatible choice. The day was depressing enough without wrapping it up in the austerity of a church that Ben didn't believe in. We wanted to play modern music that represented how Ben lived his life; therefore, the first choice was Jennifer Warnes singing *I've Had the Time of My Life*. That particular song was chosen because we all felt the title of the song reflected how Ben had lived most of his life. As the song ended, a prayer and further eulogy by Ruth followed, after which another of Ben's friends spoke. He recounted how Ben had been best man at his wedding and disclosed how he had first introduced Ben to his niece, now his fiancée.

He was followed by another one of Ben's friends who made people smile as he said, "Ben would have been pleased to see how many fit women had turned up for his funeral." I fully understood the manner in which it was said, but he was so accurate that tears began trickling down my face again. He added how Ben had lived his life to the full and how his belief was that if you want something then you should just go ahead and buy it. With that in mind, and with Ben's death reminding him of his own mortality, he concluded by saying how he had gone out and bought the car he had always wanted – as a tribute to Ben.

The next person to speak was one of Ben's RAF colleagues; again, Ben had been best man at his wedding. He commented on Ben's wicked sense of humour and on his cooking skills, which he believed to have been inherited from his father. At this point, Ruth interjected with the obligatory religious element, which served to keep the whole service grounded and mindful of why we were all there. Following Ruth's prayers, Gra and Matt were going to say a few words but Matt was too upset to stand up and talk, so Gra addressed the congregation on his own.

He began by saying he was once told that a speech should be like a woman's skirt: short enough to be interesting but long enough to cover the subject. Again, this brought some laughter from those present. He then went on to say that as the speech was for Ben, he would make it as short as possible, which was followed by more laughter. Gra then began to read the following words:

I cried the day Ben was born, the end of January 1981, a small, six pound, premature baby who spent the first ten days of his life in an incubator. I cried on the day of his passing out parade at Cranwell, on the day he got his wings. I cried on 2 September when we were told our Ben had been killed in an accident in Afghanistan. I have cried every day since, yet in between those days I have mentioned, Ben gave me no cause to cry. In fact, all I remember is happiness and laughter. You have heard from his friends what a great person he was, funny, friendly, kind, considerate, unselfish, and his fiancée tells me a hopeless romantic. To me, he was my Ben, my little lad who grew up to be a strong, sensible young man that any dad would be proud to call his son. He would tell us very little about his work in the RAF as he didn't want us to know just how dangerous it was.

He ended with a poem he wrote for Ben after his death, and a song played by Queen. He asked those present to listen carefully to the words of the song, adding that the words state how he felt about Ben leaving us all so suddenly.

To Ben
You took to the sky that fateful day, full of life and joy

You took to the sky that day, our brave boy
You didn't know it was your last, so your banter
was the same
The crew all working hard, as more height you
gained.

Our lovely boy, so high above a country far away
Our lovely boy, our Ben, our son, we sadly lost
that day
Our Ben, our precious youngest son, so lively full
of fun
He was so loved by all of us; it's hard to think he's
gone.

Ben was like a little brother all his friends agree
The best friend you could have, they have said to
me
There was only one Ben Knight, he was unique
you see
There will never be another Ben, not for you or me.

We shall always remember you, Ben, in every little
way
We will never forget you, Ben, not even for a day
We loved you, Ben, we told you so, you said you
loved us too
We want to put our arms around you, that's all we
want to do.

But go you must, you have been called to fly with
Angels now
So night night, Ben, you sleep well and our heads
we'll bow
One day perhaps we'll meet again in a land so far
away

Once more to talk and laugh with you, I look forward to that day.

Gra was in tears whilst reading the poem but he eventually managed to get to the end of it. We listened to *Love of My Life* by Queen, and when the music ended, Ruth gave a bible reading and an address followed by a few prayers. Ben's fiancée was intending to say a few words next, but she was too upset to speak so Andy spoke on her behalf, reading the words she had written down on paper. Her words were beautiful, funny and upsetting, but I have not included them here as I consider them private to her. The penultimate piece of music which followed was *You're Still the One* by Shania Twain, especially chosen by Ben's fiancée. As the song drew to a close, the RAF bearer party moved into position and carefully removed the Union flag from Ben's coffin, folding it into a triangle as they did. Next they removed Ben's hat and gloves from his coffin, placed them on the folded flag and formally presented them to his fiancée.

Ruth concluded the service with the commendation and a farewell, and as the large crematorium doors were quietly closed, Ben's coffin disappeared behind them and my Ben was gone forever. The final piece of music played, *Goodbye My Lover* by James Blunt, as the family left the large hall and gathered outside for the flypast. We were joined by the rest of the congregation, and as we all stood in the bitter cold, the heavily laden snow clouds above us released their large snowflakes. Within minutes, the crematorium grounds were swallowed up by the snow. All of a sudden, as people quietly wept and were comforted by each other, the muffled sound of an aircraft could be heard in the murky distance. As the sound neared, people strained to look beyond the dark snow clouds in order to catch a glimpse of it. If you were quick, a fleeting view of the aircraft could be seen through the falling snowflakes and spats of rain; the flypast had been barely visible, which is how Gra wanted it. As Gra and I stood alone, surrounded by so many people, desolation and despair descended upon us.

The evening gathering was at the Sergeants Mess on the airbase at Kinloss. The snow had continued to fall heavily since the end of the funeral, leaving a blanket of snow covering the RAF buildings and the open spaces. The refreshments, consisting of Ben's favourite foods, had been meticulously planned by his fiancée and cooked by staff on the airbase. Gra had had a life size poster of Ben printed so people could write messages around the edges of it. He wrote the first message so people would realise what to do. He said it would be like a memorial book for Ben's fiancée to keep. I circulated amongst the guests, thanking them for attending the funeral service and for travelling such long distances in such awful weather. I also sat with Ruth for quite a while and thanked her for all the help she had given us, although a lot of the time I was in tears. I found it comforting talking to Ruth, which was a little strange as she was the person who had delivered the worst news possible to me on 2 September 2006; but I felt a closeness to her as I felt she understood. However, Gra's experience that evening was different to mine. He found himself comforting others who were upset over Ben's death, and by the end of the day, he felt completely drained.

Now the funeral was over, I felt I would be expected to 'get on' with my life and not openly feel sad about Ben being dead. Some people had already said to me that now the funeral was over, the family needed to 'move on'. But I didn't want to move on yet... I wasn't ready to move on. I just wanted Ben to come back. If I moved on, I would feel I was leaving Ben behind and I didn't want to do that.

When the evening was over and we were back at the house in Inverness, I sat alone in the bedroom and contemplated the day's events. I hadn't wanted to organise a funeral for Ben, I loved him too much for that. I loved him so, so much. I understood him and he understood me. He knew what I meant and would smile at me when I'd say to him, "I'm always in your head."

I loved Ben and didn't want him to be dead. But he *was* dead, and everything that was happening around me just served to enforce the message that he was dead. Something that happened thousands of miles away, on the other side of the world, had changed my life forever, and I really didn't like it.

6

The Memorial Service

The memorial service was held on 29 January 2007 at RAF Kinloss and all the families of the men killed on 2 September 2006 were invited. Gra and I welcomed the chosen date, as the 28th of January would have been Ben's twenty-sixth birthday. It meant we would be at his place of work and the area where he lived for his birthday, and we were comfortable with that.

We were told by one of the other families that at the memorial service that the RAF intended to have the nose of a Nimrod protruding through into the hangar where the service was going to be held. Gra was uncomfortable with that arrangement, as were some of the other families, and in the end the RAF reluctantly admitted defeat and the idea was discarded.

Gra and I chose to stay in accommodation on the outskirts of Inverness. We wouldn't be recognisable there and could have time to ourselves. Since Ben's death, and because Gra had been outspoken with regard to safety aboard the Nimrod, we had attracted interest from the media. At the time, it may not have been immediately apparent but we were, and still are, a very private and reserved family – apart from Ben, who was very boisterous and outgoing.

On the morning of 28 January, Gra received a telephone call on his mobile from Sky News asking if they could record an interview with us. It seemed fitting for Gra and I to take part in the interview, as it would have been Ben's birthday that day and we would be able to mention that in the interview. The reporter came to the hotel, but initially our room appeared the only one available in which to conduct the interview. Gra had a word with the manager who then provided us with an empty room; we were then able to move some of the furniture around in order to accommodate the cameras. Although we didn't know the interviewer personally, we recognised her from the television news channel as she regularly reports from Scotland, so we felt at ease talking to her. We spoke about our shock and sadness at losing Ben and how it would have been his birthday that day. She asked us for our thoughts about the memorial service which was to take place the following day.

On the day of the memorial service, we had arranged to collect Matt, his partner and their seven-week-old baby from Inverness Airport before continuing on to RAF Kinloss. Their plane arrived on time, and once they were all safely in the car, we drove to the Nimrod base at RAF Kinloss. Andy also attended the service but made his own way there.

The service was to take place in one of the many aircraft hangars at the airbase. Inside the chosen hangar, a large Union flag hung with pride as it took centre stage, supported and surrounded by many colourful flowers. The Duke of Edinburgh attended the service, along with the Armed Force Minister and other politicians and officers from all three services. A senior military spokesman had announced that the service was mainly for colleagues, friends and family to say goodbye and show their respects. There were about 2,000 people who attended the service.

As we walked into the hangar where the service was to be held, the first thing that caught my attention was the sea of blue RAF uniforms. We walked between the rows of blue to our seats at the front of the congregation. It brought tears to my eyes seeing all those RAF personnel in their smart uniforms. They were just a constant reminder to me of how unfair it was that Ben was no longer alive. Why should they be here and not Ben? I would have liked to have screamed at them all to go away, to get out of my sight, for their blue uniforms taunted me terribly; it was just not fair.

When everyone had been seated, the Station Commander began by paying tribute to the fourteen men who lost their lives aboard Nimrod XV230. "Fourteen ordinary men or fourteen heroes, it matters not." He continued by saying there could be few on the airbase that did not know someone from this "band of brothers who paid the ultimate sacrifice".

The service was yet another occasion where I thought the only way I was going to get to the end of it without breaking down in tears was for me to count. In those situations, it didn't matter what I counted; sometimes I counted the number of tiles on the ceiling, sometimes the number of people in attendance, and when I had completed my counting, I would begin again. It was the only way I felt I had any control over my emotions. On this occasion, I counted the number of individual flowers on display.

The service lasted forty-five minutes, after which the families led the congregation out of the hanger. The reception afterwards was attended by the Duke of Edinburgh, RAF personnel and the families of those men who had been killed aboard Nimrod XV230 on that tragic September day. We didn't stay long at the reception. For us, there appeared to be too many people cheerily greeting each other and catching up on each others' lives. I felt the need to be away from such polite chit-chat; it all seemed too staged for me. I needed to be alone with my sorrow and sadness.

Other members of our family who had attended the service caught a flight home later that day. Gra and I stayed another night and travelled home the following day. Another chapter of this tragedy had been concluded, but there were still many more to be confronted.

7

A Crash Waiting to Happen

Gra decided that once he arrived back home in Somerset, he would endeavour to find out as much as he could about Nimrod aircraft from the internet in an attempt to understand why Ben's aircraft caught fire and exploded.

The first internet site he looked at was PPRuNe: Professional Pilots Rumour Network. He had been introduced to the site shortly after Ben's death, while we were still staying in Inverness. One of the threads on PPRuNe was entitled 'Nimrod crash in Afghanistan Tech/ Info/Discussion (NOT condolences)'. It was started on the day of the crash, and after a few days, people had already begun speculating on the possible cause of the crash and relating other fire incidents aboard Nimrod aircraft.

The first reference to fires aboard a Nimrod aircraft captured his attention immediately; it related to Nimrod XV257, which experienced a bomb bay fire on 3 June 1984. Gra read the following account in disbelief. The aircraft had taken off from its base, which at that time was RAF St Mawgan in Cornwall, and as part of its normal search and rescue (SAR) equipment, the aircraft was carrying a number of five-inch reconnaissance flares in the bomb bay. It stated that in accordance with normal practice, the first navigator switched the flare's release units to live shortly after take-off. Some thirty seconds later, a cockpit indicator warned the crew of a fire in the bomb bay. The captain immediately instructed the co-pilot to fly the aircraft back to base while he transmitted a mayday call and informed the rest of the crew. During the return flight, ground witnesses reported seeing the Nimrod trailing smoke, with several burning flares, a parachute and other objects falling from the aircraft. Fortunately, the aircraft landed safely, and although the fire services quickly extinguished the intense fire, the aircraft was extensively damaged. We later discovered other documents relating to this incident, including a report which concluded: 'The accident was caused by a reconnaissance flare becoming detached from its carrier and subsequently igniting in the bomb bay'. How the flare had come to be released could not be positively determined by the investigation team, but because of the severity of the damage to the aircraft, Nimrod XV257 had to be scrapped.

Gra wondered whether this could be what caused XV230 to crash, killing all fourteen men on board. So Nimrod XV257 became his starting point. The RAF had experienced a bomb bay fire on a Nimrod some twenty-two years earlier; Gra knew he needed to find out how the bomb bay fire was dealt with back in 1984 and whether lessons could and should have been learnt. Could the aircraft Ben was on, Nimrod XV230, have experienced the same problem as XV257 and was that the reason the aircraft caught fire and exploded?

Gra had no airworthiness or military background and realised he needed to talk to someone who did have such knowledge. He telephoned our visiting officer and asked about the flares. The VO said he would look into it and came back with an answer a couple of days later. He said the fire aboard XV230 could not have been caused by flares in the bomb bay as they would not have been carrying any flares, therefore his answer lay elsewhere. But where? Gra and I both realised, very early on, that this was going to be a long and difficult journey to establish why XV230 caught fire and who was responsible, but we were not going to be dissuaded in our search for answers by the first hurdle. Nimrod XV230 may not have suffered a bomb bay fire as first reports had suggested, but why after the fire on XV257 twenty-two years earlier had a fire suppressant system not be fitted?

In the first few weeks and months after the loss of Nimrod XV230, we knew the aircraft had caught fire because the RAF had told us so. However, we wanted to know why it caught fire, why the fire could not be extinguished, and why the aircraft exploded. We also wanted to know who was responsible. When we asked these questions to anyone within the RAF the standard answer was: "wait until the Board of Inquiry (BOI) has been completed.", But we knew that was months away, possibly even over a year away. As a family, we were all distraught over Ben's death and found it unbearable that we should have to wait so long for answers. So Gra decided that whatever it took, he would collect as much information as he could on previous 'incidents' and make himself familiar with current regulations regarding airworthiness.

Twenty very long months later, and at the end of the inquest into the fourteen deaths aboard Nimrod XV230, the Armed Force Minister said, "Some families tried to make themselves so-called experts on Nimrods" and we guessed he meant Gra. If he did mean Gra, he was right; we make no apologies that we did try to gather as much information and knowledge as possible in an attempt to unravel how and why Ben was killed.

But where were we to start? I wouldn't profess to come from a family steeped in military service and neither would Gra. I had an uncle, who passed away many years ago, who had been in the RAF and Gra's father had been in the Army. But I'm sure both had only been in the armed forces due to the Second World War and conscription, although my Uncle had remained in the RAF after the war had ended. One of my brothers had also been in the Army but more reluctantly than from his own choosing, I think, so we didn't have any relatives whom we could summon for information. The only solution was to return to the PPRuNe site on the internet, and to the Nimrod thread.

Once on the site, Gra started to note down the people he thought were Nimrod crew and which of those he suspected were maintenance staff. He read their discussions and comments carefully and tried hard to understand the jargon but soon realised that he would have to 'go public' if he was to have any chance of unravelling the real truth behind the loss of XV230. He therefore decided to join PPRuNe and registered as 'Tapper's Dad'. Within the RAF, Ben had been known as Tapper so by Gra registering as 'Tapper's Dad' he was being open and honest with the other people on the site that he was communicating with. Within a couple of weeks of joining PPRuNe, he had made some really good contacts and one in particular seemed eager to help him. Because of the nature of our enquires, and the Official Secrets Act, the names of those people who helped us have been omitted and no rank or job title has been allocated to them within this book. One of the many people who helped us greatly was someone who was able to interpret the jargon for Gra and clarify what was being said, and he supplied Gra with much of his information and knowledge. He had flown in Nimrods himself and his expertise regarding the aircraft design and airworthiness were invaluable.

We amassed further information through the Freedom of Information (FOI) Act, but usually found that the information obtained by this source needed to be used in conjunction with that which was acquired elsewhere. Of course, we didn't always get our questions answered as we had hoped. Sometimes the reply to our question would be as follows: 'It is considered that some of the information relevant to your request falls within the scope of exemption at Section 26 (Defence) of the FOI Act. Section 26 covers information which, if disclosed, would prejudice defence or the capability, effectiveness or security of relevant armed forces'. Although we understood and respected the exemption, we also realised that only the department we had contacted regarding the FOI knew if something would prejudice defence or the capability, effectiveness or security, and there was no way for us of validating their reason behind the decision. An FOI denied to us could just be another way to stop us from getting information that might prove embarrassing to the Government.

On 4 December 2006, the BBC reported that the crew of a Nimrod used a teapot to block a hatch gap in their plane after a mid-air mechanical fault. A Ministry of Defence (MOD) spokeswoman said safety had not been compromised. A Morayshire MP who has raised many questions in Parliament about the condition of the Nimrod fleet and in particular Nimrod XV230 said: "Family members of service personnel who died have had concerns about maintenance and safety. This new wave of revelations is not going to instil the crews or families with confidence. I really hope the MOD will be doing everything possible so that there are no repetitions of these technical problems and maintain safety." The MOD had promised that concerns about the safety of the RAF Nimrod fleet would be fully investigated following the September crash, and we wondered what state these aircraft were in if they needed to plug holes with a teapot! Gra made some telephone calls to a couple of the other families and they were equally dismayed and angry on hearing the teapot story. But for the time being, all we could do was continue to collect as much information regarding Nimrods, and XV230 in particular, and wait for the findings of the Board of Inquiry (BOI).

In February 2007, three weeks after the memorial

service, the *Daily Record* newspaper in Scotland had the headline 'Nimrods Grounded In Fuel Line Scare'. Apparently dents had been found in the fuel pipes of one of the aircraft, and the RAF had grounded the rest of the fleet while checks were made. I and some of the other relatives commented in the newspapers that we were shocked, for these aircraft were all supposed to have been checked following the crash as it was a possibility the crash was caused by a leaking fuel pipe. Now, five months after those checks, this latest issue was discovered, and it was serious enough to ground the fleet.

A few weeks later, in March, there was an article in *The Times* newspaper which stated, 'RAF rebels quit over fuel danger in ageing spy plane'. The newspaper said that they had received emails from aircrew at RAF Kinloss disclosing that there had been six fuel leaks on board Nimrods since the loss of XV230 in September 2006. Sources, identified as Nimrod crew members, were quoted as saying, "It's not a nice place to work just now" and that "confidence in both the aircraft and the hierarchy is at an all time low". They expressed concern about the number of fuel leaks and the 'hurry to resume air-to-air refuelling' attitude after each leak. Gra telephoned a number of the other relatives to talk to them and they too appeared distressed and angry that these aircraft were still flying even though they appeared not to be safe.

Our sources of information will always remain anonymous, but we will always be grateful for the help and information they provided for us. What initially started as a trickle of information about Nimrod incidents quickly became a torrent, and Gra found himself spending longer and longer trying to make sense of it all. By now, he had twelve box files that were quickly being filled with paperwork relating to and connecting with Nimrod XV230. The largest bundle of papers was the file on Nimrod incidents. The information in that file came to him from sources within the RAF and also from FOI requests. One such document requested under the FOI Act was a list of incidents affecting Nimrod aircraft from the first in-service flight up to the day of the crash. This one document proved to be his 'Rosetta Stone'.

When it duly arrived by email, Gra began to categorise the incidents, and as he did, he started to get a sick feeling in the pit of his stomach. The document contained details of 2,496 incidents affecting RAF Nimrod aircraft from 1987–2007, an average of 124 incidents a year! The RAF categorise an aircraft incident as an occurrence involving an aircraft which results in the aircraft sustaining damage or a person receiving an injury, or which discloses a flight safety hazard or potential hazard. On breaking down the figures, alarm bells started to ring; this airframe appeared to have many problems. The loss of Nimrod XV230 was quickly presenting itself as an accident waiting to happen. There had been 355 incidents of fumes/smoke, Nimrods had suffered 377 reported leaks, 32 incidents of fuel contamination and 11 incidents relating to fuel transfer problems. As if all that wasn't bad enough, there were 299 incidents of equipment failing to operate, 184 incidents of parts detaching and a further fifty-five incidents of structural damage to aircraft. There had also been eight fuel transfer probe leaks.

As Gra sat staring at the figures, the sick feeling inside him increased until he slowly began to cry. He called me to come and look at the figures but I was more concerned that he was upset and I asked him what was wrong. "Look," he said. "Look at that... seventy-eight fires and 355 incidents of fume and smoke. It's wrong, it's so wrong. They must have known these aircraft were not safe."

I looked over his shoulder at the figures and asked him if he was sure the figures were correct but he said he was; he'd looked at them again and again, as much in disbelief as for any other reason. Tears also came to my eyes as I said to Gra, "It's their fault, isn't it? They killed Ben." We hugged each other, both realising the significance of what we had just been reading but at the same time not knowing what we could do about it. It didn't seem right that the general public were being kept in the dark about the many faults on these aircraft.

Gra decided to telephone one of the people who had been providing us with an enormous amount of help and whose support had been there for us from the very beginning of this continuing nightmare. We first met at a pub in Forres a few months after the loss of XV230. Gra had gone to the bar to buy the drinks and I had sat with him and cried as I proceeded to inform him of the state of Ben's body. He sat quietly as he listened to my anguish and I thank him immensely for allowing me to say what I did that day. Mentally, I have come a long, long way since that day. The fact that Ben is dead and I will never, ever see him again still upsets me, but my mental health has moved forward.

So Gra spoke with him over the telephone and explained the facts and figures to him. He was equally shocked and disgusted and it was agreed that the information needed to be placed in the public domain. It was no good waiting for the Board of Inquiry to report; there was no guarantee they would refer to the incidents, and they may even try to cover them up. But as one incident after another was revealed to us, it also left us asking even more questions and a further FOI would usually be requested from the MOD. It was a paper chase; every time Gra requested information, the reply would point him in the direction of other incidents and reports that were just as important, if not more, than the last one.

There were three documents that would prove to be of great significance during 2007, the first being an incident report relating to Nimrod XV227. On 22 November 2004,

XV227 was being flown on a 42 (Reserve) Squadron training sortie which appeared uneventful and the aircraft returned to RAF Kinloss without incident. The ground crew commenced their normal servicing and discovered a rupture in the aircraft system, known as the Supplementary Conditioning Pack (SCP) duct. Put simply, a hot air pipe (the SCP) ruptured and air heated to 400 degrees Celsius escaped and had heated the fuel in one of the numerous fuel tanks to boiling point. The official incident report detailed damage to the aircraft resulting from the incident, this included damage to the airframe structure, coupling, seals and wiring looms. As a result, the Aircraft Ground Engineer declared the aircraft unserviceable. The incident report made seven recommendations, including that a maintenance policy be introduced, that the ruptured ducts be replaced fleet wide and that a hot air leak warning system be introduced to cover all possible duct failures. It was also noted that the mission system recorder was unreliable and may have led to valuable evidence being lost. The incident involving XV227 in November 2004 was very significant and would be referred to again and again at the inquest, because it was the same SCP component on XV230 that failed, causing hot air to ignite fuel and kill fourteen men. If the MOD and RAF had implemented the recommendations resulting from the XV277 incident then our son may have still been alive today.

Sometime later, Gra received a set of emails from one of his many anonymous sources. Although they could not be used at the coroner's inquest as they were not obtained legally, they proved to be of great interest as they offered an insight into the response at RAF Kinloss to the increasing number of fuel leak incidents affecting the Nimrod fleet. The emails spanned the period 2 December 2005 to 15 February 2006 and made specific reference to fuel leaks on board XV230. One such email referred to the 'leak headache' and another said that they needed to decide whether they would 'tackle the leaks properly' or 'limp the aircraft through using patch repairs' until its out of service date. The out of service date is the date when the aircraft should no longer be flying, which at that time, having been deferred yet again, was 2009.

Of all the documents that we obtained in our search for the truth behind the loss of XV230, a safety report produced by BAE Systems would prove to be the most valuable. BAE were responsible for the maintenance and servicing of the Nimrod fleet and had been commissioned by the RAF to complete a safety case on the airframe. The report was submitted to the RAF in 2004 and highlighted a number of safety concerns with the Nimrod fleet and made recommendations to address these concerns. BAE recommended the fitting of a fire suppression system in the bomb bay, warning that failure to do so could result in an uncontrollable fire leading to the loss of an aircraft. They also recommended that the RAF keep a watching brief on fuel tank protection directives in the commercial aviation sector. Most significantly, they highlighted the supply of hot air to the SCP as a cause for concern; it warned that hot air pipes adjacent to fuel pipes/tanks could act as a source of ignition. In addition, BAE recommended that nitrogen inerting systems should be seriously considered for all new and in-service aircraft to prevent the build up of explosive vapour in a partially empty fuel tank.

On 2 September 2006, leaking fuel was said to have dripped onto the SCP duct on board Nimrod XV230, igniting it and causing a catastrophe. To the best of our knowledge, not one of the recommendations in the BAE report of 2004 had been implemented. The incorporation of a fire suppression system was rejected on the grounds that the MOD believed it would be ineffective. In my view, in respect of most of the recommendations, the RAF and

MOD simply appeared to have ignored the advice of BAE Systems.

The significance of the SCP duct cannot be overstated. Gra was sure the RAF and MOD had a whole manual describing the function of the SCP duct, but in simple terms it cools down the cabin, making it more comfortable for the crew. In a report received by the RAF in 2005, relating to the corroded hot air duct (SCP) on XV227, it was recommended that Nimrod aircraft were inspected to establish what similar ducts were in the same condition. The defence contractors QinetiQ were commissioned to undertake this work and it took them two years to complete their report after inspecting just two aircraft. When XV230 crashed, the SCP system was still in operation on Nimrod aircraft, but immediately after the crash, it was disabled. There was no cost to disabling the SCP, other than the crew being a little warmer, and it had no effect on the aircraft capabilities. Crucially, however, if the 2004 BAE recommendations had been addressed and the 2005 QinetiQ inspections had been completed fleet wide, then Ben may still have been alive today.

Gra and I were cross and upset when we uncovered this information. Our son was dead, and it could have been prevented. The RAF and the MOD had not just missed one warning sign; they appeared to have missed or chosen to ignore numerous warnings and recommendations that may have prevented the loss of XV230. In all the reports and evidence we had collected, everything screamed out that the Nimrod was a tired, old aircraft that was an accident waiting to happen. Who was responsible for making the decision to continue using the SCP system after the 2004 incident on XV227? We needed to find that information out.

Gra had to admit that he knew nothing about Nimrods before the crash of Ben's aircraft; in fact, he knew nothing about any aircraft. We were not a military family, and although initially that made it difficult for him to understand the workings and maintenance of an aircraft, it also helped in that he was not fazed by the military stance and the hierarchy system within it. He was not afraid to ask a question of someone just because they were an Air Chief Marshall, or some other high rank, for rank meant nothing to him. It didn't impress him, nor did it fluster him. Now that he had all this information pointing towards serious problems within the Nimrod fleet and XV230 in particular, we had to decide what to do with it all. By now, more and more people were offering us help, information, knowledge and experience, and often Gra would contact one of his main contacts for further assistance. We can't thank these people enough for all their support and advice, for without them we wouldn't have even been able to understand the language of the RAF or the details of the incidents. Our biggest fear was that of a whitewash by the BOI, so we decided that we had enough evidence of bad practice to release some of the information to the media. Many of the newspapers were supportive of our intention to expose the true facts about airworthiness within the RAF; therefore, we had no shortage of outlets when we felt we needed them. In the weeks following the loss of XV230, many journalists from television, radio and the newspapers had been in contact with us and provided us with a contact number should we want to share any information with them. Some of the newspapers were also carrying out their own investigations regarding XV230 and a number of them quite often produced articles about the latest findings regarding Nimrods. One such article in the *Sunday Times* on 2 April 2007 entitled 'MOD accused of cost-cutting on crash plane' included details of an incident, post-September 2006, when a Nimrod reportedly landed with seven tons of aviation fuel sloshing around in the bomb bay.

On 3 June 2007, the BBC *Panorama* programme covered the Nimrod crash and the fleet wide problem regarding safety. Gra had provided the BBC with some of the material that he had obtained. However, we believe the main source of information for the programme was an RAF whistleblower with twenty years experience as an airman. He stated that there were deep concerns among service personnel about the poor state of the Nimrod fleet. Reference was made to numerous technical faults and fuel leaks, including an incident during a Nimrod flight in UK airspace in November 2004. The whistleblower believed that the incident could have brought down the aircraft involved. Photographs of the damage were passed to the programme; they showed scorching below the wing fuel tanks and in the bomb bay of the aircraft. The whistleblower revealed that a hot air pipe (SCP) had ruptured below the fuel tanks and that superheated air had 'blasted out' melting the fuel pipe seals. He also said, "Chances are, if they had flown for a few more hours, we would have lost them, and yet the aircrew knew nothing about what was happening. It was only when they landed that it was discovered."

On the first anniversary of the crash of Nimrod XV230, the *Sunday Times* published an article under the headline 'MOD rejected fire safety plan for doomed Nimrod'. The article referred to the BAE safety case document that Gra had obtained and stated that BAE had recommended in 2004 that a fire detection and suppression system be fitted in the Nimrod bomb bays. The MOD rejected the recommendation on the basis that they claimed it was unlikely to be effective. This *Sunday Times* article was the beginning of a burst of activity and interest from the press in late 2007 as expectations grew that the Board of Inquiry (BOI) would soon publish its findings.

In October 2007, several articles appeared in the UK press. The headlines speak for themselves: 'Emails show

RAF knew of crash plane fuel leaks', reported the *Daily Telegraph*. The *Daily Mirror* published an article headed 'Deadly Nimrod danger ignored'; and having been provided with information by Gra on corrosion problems with the Nimrod fleet (information given to him by a BAE insider), the *Independent* reported 'Revealed: secret report on Britain's rusty spy planes'. It included numerous documents that Gra had passed out to media outlets and consisted of leaked emails that he had received. Later in that October, the *Times* reported 'RAF knew that crashed Nimrod had dangerous fuel leak record'. The following day, the *Sunday Times* said 'Spy plane sent to war with fatal flaw'. We hoped that all this press coverage would put pressure on the RAF and MOD and ensure that they could not whitewash the truth.

The pressure on the RAF and MOD continued into November, as a potentially catastrophic fuel leak took place on board a Nimrod high above Afghanistan. On 8 November, the *Daily Telegraph* said 'Nimrod in Mayday over fuel leak' and the *Daily Mirror* said 'Terror of Nimrod fuel leak'. More than a year after the loss of XV230, a Nimrod flying an ISTAR (Intelligence, Surveillance, Target acquisition and Reconnaissance) mission over Afghanistan made a mayday call when fuel began to pour into the bomb bay during refuelling. Unlike Nimrod XV230, this time the aircraft was able to land safely at Kandahar. A few days later, the *Observer* published a story based on a report produced by Qinetiq that Gra had obtained and passed on to the newspaper. Under the headline 'MOD accused over spy plane deaths', it said an internal defence report highlighted a catalogue of 'critical' failings during an investigation into the recurrent problem of fuel leaks within the Nimrod fleet. The report raised deep-rooted concerns about a 'low standard of workmanship' and 'inadequate' training of mechanics. It said that these issues where first brought to their attention about seven years earlier in 1999, but Qinetiq concluded that there was no evidence that the issues had been rectified or addressed.

Finally, at the end of November, another article in the *Observer* newspaper underlined the seriousness of the problems within the Nimrod fleet and the RAF and MOD's apparent inability to address them. On 25 November 2007, the paper reported that there had been 880 fires on RAF Nimrods before the loss of Nimrod XV230.

Gra and I felt we had done all we could to expose the catalogue of incidents and fuel leaks affecting the Nimrod fleet. We had helped highlight numerous errors, missed opportunities and bad judgment calls by the RAF and MOD. All we could do now was wait for the BOI to publish its findings.

8

Killed By His Own Side – The Board Of Inquiry

On a drab November morning in 2007, we received another starched white envelope from Headquarters No 2 Group, Royal Air Force, High Wycombe. The neat letter inside informed us that the Board of Inquiry into the loss of Nimrod XV230 had been concluded and that the report would be released to the families and public on 4 December 2007.

The letter stated that the Secretary of State for Defence was required to make a formal statement in the House of Commons on the day of the release, however, shortly before that the families would be provided with a redacted copy of the report. It went on to explain that a redaction was carried out in order to remove operationally sensitive detail from the report to ensure the continued safety of our servicemen and women on operations, and to remove sensitive personal information. The letter outlined the two options available to us with regard to receiving and discussing the report.

The first option was that we could receive the report at home, where our VO and a specialist from within the RAF would take us through the content of the report and answer any questions that we may have. Although we would be able to ask any questions we wanted to, it was pointed out that some questions may need to be taken away with an answer provided at a later date, which we perfectly understood.

The second option was the opportunity to travel to London and receive a private, individual briefing and a copy of the report on the morning of 4 December in much the same manner as outlined above. However, after the private briefing, we would have the added opportunity to travel to the Ministry of Defence in Whitehall to take part in a group meeting, along with the other families. The meeting, with the President of the BOI, would try and answer any technical questions we may want to put before them. In addition, the Minister of State for the Armed Forces and the Chief of Air Staff, an Air Chief Marshall, would be making themselves available later in the day to discuss any further questions people may have. The letter concluded by informing us that at the end of the afternoon, a media facility would be made available for any families who may wish to make a statement to the press.

Gra and I, and the other members of our family, had been waiting fifteen long months for the BOI findings to be released and we were initially hoping it would at last explain why Ben's aircraft caught fire and exploded. We also wanted to know who was responsible for the loss of Nimrod XV230 and more importantly the deaths of those on board. For Ben's family, it had seemed like a very long wait, and at last, we hoped to get some answers.

Unfortunately, after a fifteen month wait, the selected release date of the BOI was 4 December 2007, the date of our only grandchild's first birthday. (We now have three more grandchildren.) Baby Callum's mother had been six months pregnant when Ben was killed, and he was a very special addition to the Knight family at a time when we were experiencing some of our darkest days. Gra and I didn't feel it would be right for us to travel up to London from Somerset and miss his first birthday. A first birthday is very special – it cannot be revisited. We both felt Ben would totally understand our decision to stay in Somerset. We would then be able to hear the BOI findings at our home with the support of our VO and still be able visit Callum on the afternoon of his momentous first birthday. In addition, the day following the BOI findings release, our other two sons, Andy and Matt, and their partners were flying off on holiday to the Canaries and it had been arranged well in advance of the BOI date being fixed that we would be available to drive them to the airport.

We replied to the RAF letter explaining our decision, and so it was agreed that our VO and an RAF engineer would arrive at our house at 10.00am on 4 December 2007 to talk us through our copy of the BOI and, hopefully, explain why Ben was killed.

The MOD issued a press release inviting members of the press to a 'lock-in' on Tuesday 4 December 2007 at the media suite of the MOD Main Building, Whitehall, in London for those wishing to attend. A lock-in, I understand, is just as it implies. If you agree to attend, then you are locked in between the given times and are not allowed access to those outside the lock-in until the end. I also believe mobiles phones cannot be used by those at the lock-in. This prevents the media and press from reporting the details before the announcement in Parliament and before the families have been informed. Members of the press wanting to attend were informed to enter the press suite via a separate entrance to the left-hand side of the main entrance. They were also informed that they would have to provide a valid press pass or similar photo identification, without which access would not be given.

The lock-in was set to begin at 12.15pm, when those present would receive a redacted copy of the Board of Inquiry findings plus background material. A presentation by the BOI President on the Board's findings would be given, followed by a question and answer session. After a short break, the Secretary of State would begin his statement to the House of Commons on the findings of the BOI which would be relayed live to the MOD media suite, and at that time, anyone requesting to leave the lock-in would be able to do so.

The day after the press release was circulated, our telephone seemed to ring constantly. Newspapers, television and radio stations were all trying to contact us, wanting to know if we would be going to London to hear the BOI findings. When we told them that we were staying in Somerset and having the BOI findings explained to us at home, they immediately asked if they could come to our house and interview us afterwards. Over the months, the media had given us so much help and coverage as we tried to find out the truth about why XV230 caught fire and exploded that Gra just said yes to everyone, not really knowing whether any of them would opt for sleepy Somerset over the hustle and bustle of London and Parliament. However, if any of them did choose sleepy Somerset, he informed them that he would not be able to speak with them until 12.00 noon at the very earliest.

The day before the release of the BOI findings, Gra and I were both slightly apprehensive; neither of us knew quite what to expect from the report. Since the loss of XV230, Gra had worked fervently in an attempt to unravel the true facts of why the aircraft exploded and who was responsible. In our opinion, some individuals from organizations such as the MOD and the RAF had tried to block our path in the quest for the whole truth; however, many more had wanted to help us and provided us with so much information that we will be eternally grateful and appreciative of the risks they took in doing so.

As we considered retiring to our bed for the night on the eve of the BOI release, Slade were merrily singing *Merry Christmas Everybody* on the television. I thought how immense the contrast was between a happy Christmas and our present lives as we prepared to face a second Christmas without Ben.

We didn't sleep well that night. With so many scenarios swishing through our heads, we awoke early the following morning, both wondering what news the day would bring. We had waited so long for this day, but now that it had arrived, I felt cautious and slightly apprehensive. Were we looking at a potential whitewash by the RAF and MOD? They were certainly capable of suppressing information if they so wished to; all we could do was wait.

At 8.30am, we received a telephone call from our VO asking if it would be convenient for him and his colleague to arrive at our house a little earlier than first planned. We agreed, thinking the sooner this painful process started the better. At 9.30am, our VO and his colleague arrived, carrying two large books and a folder between them. As I let them into the house, I could see that there were already satellite television vans and press beginning to gather in the street outside. Our VO introduced his colleague to us and we all took our seats. His colleague explained to us that they would first read through a document of some fifteen pages titled 'Families Brief' and afterwards we could ask any questions. We were then passed our copy of the said document, which Gra and I opened immediately and began reading. It was a very emotional and agonizing time for us, and almost from the start of reading, we became upset and irritated.

On the first page it was stated that:

> *Because of the nature of the crash and its location, the evidence presented to the Board of Inquiry was incomplete and some required considerable restoration. Despite extensive research and consideration, the Board was unable to determine positively what led to the loss of XV230, but it has been able to put forward a probable cause, which is supported by the evidence.*

It went on to discuss the record of events on 2 September 2006 and how, until the completion of air-to-air refuelling, everything had appeared normal on the aircraft with no problems being reported. It wasn't until 11.11:33 that a bomb bay fire warning, 'followed immediately by an elevator bay under floor smoke warning', was reported on the crew intercom. The times are taken from the transcript of the cockpit voice recorder found at the crash site and are accurate to the second.

Out of respect for Ben and his colleagues, I do not think it is appropriate to detail what followed next on the aircraft, I'll just say that six minutes and six seconds later a 'Harrier pilot reported that he saw the Nimrod explode at an assessed height of approximately 3000 feet above the ground'. The report went on to state that 'the crew were killed instantly'.

We continued reading the Families Brief but now in conjunction with the Board of Inquiry report where there was much discussion regarding fuel pipes and couplings. The report stated:

The Board concluded that a leak of engine bleed air could have caused disruption to the fuel system, either to a fuel coupling on the refuel pipe work or to a seal on the front face of No 7 tank, leading to a fuel leak when AAR pressurized the system: thus, such a fault is a possible cause of XV230's fire and, thus, of the loss of the aircraft.

Gra and I looked at each other in dismay, for this is what we had feared all along. The previous incident aboard XV227 could have happened again. Rather than wait for the report from Qinetiq on the SCP (hot air pipe), the RAF had allowed the SCP to be switched back on after the XV227 incident, seemingly casting aside any concerns regarding safety. Gra commented to our VO's colleague, raising his disquiet at what he was reading and wanting to know what the final conclusion was. We were referred to the remarks from senior officers in the main report. Air Chief Marshal Sir Clive Loader, Commander-in-Chief Air Command, said in his comments in the BOI report:

I conclude that the loss of XV230 and, far more importantly, of the fourteen service personnel who were aboard resulted from shortcomings in the application of the processes for assuring airworthiness and safe operation of the Nimrod.

As we continued reading the BOI report and the Families Brief, Gra looked up at the two RAF men and with tears in his eyes said, "So, his aircraft wasn't airworthy then. Is that what he is saying?"

They both looked despondent as one nodded and the other quietly replied, "It looks like that."

At this point, Gra found it overwhelming and retired to his office and cried. I continued to sit on the sofa and thought about Ben and the rest of the crew, and how it must have been for them as the smoke and flames quickly spread. Was Ben scared? I hoped not; the thought of Ben being scared in those final few minutes aboard XV230 is really too much for us to endure and we have always tried not to dwell on that point.

Gra's 'beautiful boy' and 'my Ben', killed in an un-airworthy aircraft possibly due to the RAF not doing enough after other incidents had occurred. The warning signs had long been there, but they had just been missed or not realized. It seemed that priorities had not been prioritized correctly, and as a result, Ben had been killed. People were apologetic now, but what good was that to us?, No good at all, because however you looked at this tragic situation – and whatever reasons people put forward for the failings – the end result could never be changed. Ben was dead and would always remain so.

Gra returned to the lounge, wiping away tears as he did so, and continued reading the BOI report and the Families Brief with me. Further reading just strengthened our belief that Ben's death had been avoidable.

The Board of Inquiry summarized the causes and factors in relation to the loss of XV230. However, because so little of the aircraft had been recovered from the crash site, it stated, 'the Board has been unable to determine positively the source or cause of the fire which led o the loss of XV230 and its crew'. However, through careful investigation of the data that was available, the Board gave their opinion of where they believed the fire most probably started and its causes.

It was proposed that escaped fuel catching fire was the initial cause of the fire, suggesting that fuel overflow from the No 1 tank or leakage from a fuel coupling or pipe led to an accumulation of fuel which ignited following contact with an exposed cross feed/SCP pipe. Possible contributory factors were cited as:

a) The age of the Nimrod MR2's non-structural system components. b) Nimrod MR2 maintenance policy in relation to fuel and hot air systems. c) The lack of a fire detection and suppression system within the No 7 tank dry bay. d) The fact that hazard analysis did not correctly categorize the potential threat to the aircraft caused by the collocation of fuel and hot air system components within the No 7 tank dry bay. e) Formal incorporation of AAR capability within the Nimrod did not identify the full implications of successive changes to the fuel system and associated procedures.

Eventually, when we had finished reading the Families Brief and glanced through the pages of the BOI report – because the size and content of the BOI report required a few days reading and time to digest its contents – there seemed nothing more to ask of our VO's colleague. It was therefore agreed not to take up any more of his time and let him leave and return to the hotel he was staying at. Our VO stayed with us.

It was now midday, and when the waiting press that were gathered outside saw the RAF man leave the house, an unstoppable tide of cameras and reporters surged towards our drive, all wanting to know the result of the Board of Inquiry and our response. The sudden amount of media people was too overwhelming for me at first. I had sat with incredible sorrow and listened to the explanation of how my youngest child had been killed, but I was also conscious that the BOI had presented more questions than answers.

I suddenly decided it was time I went to visit my grandchild on his first birthday. Anything anyone else had to say about Ben could wait, as none of it was going to make any difference whatsoever. Ben was dead and no one could bring him back to life. He would remain dead forever; it didn't matter how many words were spoken about what had happened to the aircraft and who was at fault, Ben would always remain dead. I was still very unhappy, upset and inwardly cross at his death.

Matt only lived a short distance away so I said to the VO, "Come on, we're going to Matt's," and we left the house together. Gra could deal with the media frenzy in the street, which spilt out from the many reporters' cars and satellite broadcasting vans that crowded around our house all vying for the best position and the opportunity to secure the first interview from him. However, he soon realised that there were so many people requesting he speak with them first that he eventually decided to invite them all inside the house, where they could divide themselves between the two lounges and decide amongst themselves in what order they would conduct the interviews.

While they set up their cameras and equipment, searching for electric sockets and suitable lighting, Gra saw it as the perfect opportunity to excuse himself from their presence and retire into the peacefulness of the back garden for a much-needed cigarette. A few minutes later, refreshed by his cigarette, he returned to the house and proceeded to make himself a cup of tea in kitchen. The Defence Secretary was soon to make a televised statement in the House of Commons with regard to the Board of Inquiry findings and Gra was expected to comment live on the statement to the waiting media. He felt he needed a little time to himself to gather his thoughts and feelings on the extraordinary events of the day, but the whole ground floor of our house appeared completely taken over by the media and their cameras.

As the statement in the House of Commons drew to a close, the media were eagerly awaiting Gra's response and their story. Gra spoke to Sky TV first, who had set their camera up in one room. Immediately afterwards, he spoke to the BBC who were in another room. He then returned to the first room to speak to ITN. There were also newspaper journalists in the house, as well as radio broadcasters, all wanting to speak with Gra and hear his views on the BOI report and the statement made in Parliament. Gra recalled afterwards that there was so much going on and so many different people in our house, coupled with the anticipation and emotion of it all, that it became a bit of a blur to him as the afternoon wore on. He told them the BOI report contained all his worst fears come true and confirmed that fourteen innocent men had lost their lives due to the incompetence of others, and that if people had put their responsibilities before their careers, then Ben would still be alive.

Gra was very upset and cross that day, but his aim was to hold back his tears until all the media people had packed up their belongings and left the house. Ben was dead, killed by the very people who should have been supporting him. Gra wanted to know who these people were and what action was going to be taken against them. With frustration and tears mounting, the time seemed right for another cigarette break so out into the garden he went again, leaving the house to the mercy of the press.

I arrived back from Matt's house, accompanied by our VO, shortly after Gra had given one of his many interviews to the media about his response to the BOI report. His sister, Lesley, was also at our house. She had anticipated that the day would be very busy for us and had volunteered to come over and just 'be there' and make tea as required. We were both very grateful for her support. As I entered our house, someone who shortly introduced himself as one of the many reporters at the house asked politely who I was. I was somewhat disorientated by his welcome, for surely in my own house it should be me asking that question of him, not the other way around. I gave him a puzzled look and told him I was "Trish, Gra's wife" and then walked through to the computer room, stepping over leads and around reporters, to find Gra. He was busy talking to another reporter, but when they eventually finished their conversation, I explained to him my strange encounter as I entered the house. Although predominantly it was a sad and stressful day, at the end of it we did smile as I recalled that incident.

There seemed to be so many people in our house – some were setting up cameras and talking about camera angles, others were hurriedly making notes in little notebooks and busily chatting to one another. Between themselves, they also openly discussed which one of them would conduct the next interview, deciding whether to talk to Gra, myself, or the two of us together; adding that if one of them interviewed Gra, then the other could interview me. It was a very surreal situation, and amidst it all, Ben was still dead. The TV people wanted to film Gra watching the Defence Secretary on the television as he began reading his statement to the House of Commons, which was being broadcast live. However, the day had been so busy that neither of us had had much to eat, and Gra was feeling the need for sustenance before he did any more interviews. I retired to the kitchen, the only ground floor space that was not totally occupied by the media, and endeavoured to put together a sandwich for him accompanied by a cup of tea. I thought it only polite to ask all the 'guests' if they too would like a drink, and then panicked as I set about searching for enough matching cups amongst a collection of crockery that normally only supported the two of us.

Later in the day, Matt came to the house to see how we were and decided that he would watch the speech from the House of Commons with Gra. When they switched on the television, the mood in the House of Commons appeared subdued. Within minutes, the Defence Secretary stood on his feet and began his sombre speech:

It is clear to me that some of the findings of the Board of Inquiry identify failings for which the Ministry of Defence must take responsibility. On behalf of the MOD and the Royal Air Force, I would like to say sorry for those failings to the House, but most of all to the families of those who lost their lives.

It was quite difficult and distressing listening to that statement for as it unravelled, so too did the painful realization that Ben need not have died, that he could still have been alive today if only people had done their jobs properly. It left me with a feeling of sadness and anger.

125

The statement continued:

I recognise that the Board of Inquiry report will be painful reading for many, but I hope that the families and friends will take some comfort in finding answers to many of the questions that arise after an incident such as this.

We thought what an inappropriate and insensitive thing to say – that we may 'take some comfort in finding answers to many of the questions...' Yes, we did need answers to our questions and we considered ourselves entitled to them, but no *comfort* came with them, just the very, very sad realisation that Ben need not have died. Everything I read in the BOI report and everything that was said in the Defence Secretary's statement that day just served to emphasise the fact that Ben did not have to die, and there is certainly no comfort attached with the realisation of that fact.

Gra gave his responses in his interviews as we both continued to shake our heads in disbelief and sadness. I wondered what Ben would have thought of it all and whether he was watching from wherever he was; he must have felt even more let down and betrayed than we did. I loved him so much.

As the afternoon surrendered to the early evening, our house continued to be occupied by people not known to me. I felt a stranger in my own home. With a sudden urge of irritation, I decided I needed to know who these people occupying my private living space were. I addressed each one of them in turn, questioning their name and which television company, newspaper or radio station they were from. That done, I settled myself down on the settee again and watched from the perimeter as my life played out before me, courtesy of the media. Eventually, with their interviews recorded, they slowly began to pack away their equipment and gradually leave, allowing the house to return to some sort of normality,

There were many unanswered phone messages that needed our attention. While the media filled our house, we had tended to ignore the phones, only answering the occasional call and usually just jotting down a name and number with the promise that we would return their call as soon as we were free. I was now faced with numerous scraps of paper with hurriedly written numbers on them and incomplete names. I attempted to recall each one of them to Gra for his attention. It was not until 10.15pm, when all the scraps of paper and their numbers had been attended to and the recipients dutifully contacted, that Gra and I were able to sit down together and assess the day's events.

Prior to that day, we had thought that after the release of the BOI report our waiting for answers would be drawing to a close. However, the Defence Secretary had also announced in the House of Commons that a review into the loss of Nimrod XV230 was to be undertaken by an eminent QC, who would also examine the wider airworthiness process within the RAF. He was to have at his disposal technical experts on aviation systems and the authority to travel to whichever country he chose in his pursuit of 'the broader issues surrounding the loss of... XV230'. The families of those who died aboard XV230 were to be kept up to date with how the review was progressing at regular intervals and a contact telephone number would be provided to them.

As the day drew to a close, we sat exhausted in the lounge, talking about the day's events and preparing to face a second Christmas without Ben. The BOI had provided us with some answers but had left us asking even more questions.

9

Lies and Liability – The Inquest

Gra had first turned his thoughts towards the inquest a few months after Ben had been killed. Initially, we did not understand that the Board of Inquiry had to present their findings before the inquest could take place, nor did we know in much detail what happens at an inquest, who can attend and who else will be present. He had read in newspapers that one of the main issues bereaved families of service personnel encounter was the bewilderment of attending the inquest into their loved one's death, whilst knowing very little about the formal process. Like the majority of the public, we were not in a financial position to be able to afford the services of a quality solicitor, but realised we would need quality legal representation when we came face to face with the MOD at the inquest. The only answer was to find an eminent solicitor who would represent us on a pro bono basis, which meant they would represent us without any cost to ourselves.

Thank goodness we now live in an age of computers and the internet, for locating a pro bono solicitor without the use of a computer must be a near impossible task. However, all Gra had to do was type in 'pro bono solicitors', click on *search* and he was presented with a selection of names. He also typed in 'Nimrod', and half way down the first page was a name of a solicitors and a piece of writing about the Nimrod crash. He made a note of their name, Irwin Mitchell Solicitors, and then went on to their website in order to find out more about the company. The website revealed that they had represented a number of military families at inquests previously, so Gra made a note of their telephone number and decided to phone them.

As he waited for someone to lift the receiver at the solicitor's office and respond to his call, he was slightly apprehensive of what awaited him. We had not been in this situation before, thank goodness, and this was all new territory for us. When a polite and soft-spoken voice at the other end of the phone greeted him, he introduced himself and explained briefly our situation and predicament. He was surprised at their response for he was told that they had heard about the crash of Nimrod XV230 and that they also recognised his name from the newspapers and television. Gra was unsure whether the latter half of their response was a good thing or not, and held his breath as the call was transferred to a more senior member of the company.

After discussions with the second person, Gra was relieved to hear that the company would indeed be able to represent us at the inquest on a pro bono basis. The man on the end of the telephone asked if any of the other families would be requesting legal representation as well. We had not discussed our intentions with any of the other relatives as we didn't really know them. The only connection we had with them was that we had all lost loved ones in the same air crash. Apart from that, we didn't have a bond with any of them in the first few months following the crash other than Ben's fiancée. As the months past by, we did form friendships with some of the other families and many of them did decide to use that same solicitor. Eventually, I think all the families but one chose to be represented at the inquest by the solicitor Gra had found all those months earlier.

It was agreed with the solicitor that he would keep in contact with us while we awaited the outcome of the RAF

Board of Inquiry (BOI), which was certainly many months away from that initial telephone conversation. However, quite soon after the BOI had presented their findings in December 2007, we received a letter from the Solicitor. The letter informed us of a pre-hearing meeting at the Coroner's Court in Oxford, which was to take place on 14 January 2008. It was suggested that the families wishing to be represented by Irwin Mitchell Solicitors meet at the Coroner's Court an hour-and-a-half before the court proceedings were due to begin in order to have time to discuss what would be happening in court later.

As the families and next of kin lived as far away as Inverness and Cornwall, travelling to Oxford was going to be a long journey for many of them. However, we were informed by the RAF that they would pay for one night's accommodation and travel expenses for those families wishing to attend the pre-inquest dates. Somerset to Oxford is just a couple of hours drive for us, and it made a welcome change to driving from Somerset all the way up to RAF Kinloss or Inverness in the north of Scotland – a journey we had done on so many occasions as we struggled to deal with the necessities that surround a sudden and unexpected death.

For the first pre-inquest date, Gra and I decided to travel to Oxford the evening before, ensuring that we arrived in plenty of time for the meeting with the solicitor the following morning. The hotel and rooms had been booked in advance by the RAF and the details and directions posted to us in a letter. The journey, past the tranquil fields of Wiltshire as opposed to the din of the motorway, took us a couple of hours and we arrived at the hotel at about 7.00pm. As Gra is a smoker, something that I persistently badger him about, he was a little disappointed that we had not been allocated a smoking room; this was before the smoking ban came into being and when smoking was still permitted in public places. Our car was parked a short distance away from the hotel so Gra decided to stand on the doorstep of a side entrance of the hotel to indulge in his smoking habit. While he stood there alone, the next of kin of one of the other crew members aboard XV230 joined him and they began talking. Although we had noticed her from meetings held at RAF Kinloss, the Repatriation Ceremony and the memorial service, we had not been in a position to talk with her before. Now, she introduced herself to Gra and the two of them seemed to get on well. We knew that Ben had been a friend of her son and that Ben had lived just a few houses away from his girlfriend. As Gra and the lady continued their conversation, he arranged for the two of us to walk with her the following day the short distance to the Coroner's Court.

The Oxford Coroner's Court was a revelation to us. We had viewed the outside of the building many times on the television as reporters stood outside the large doors interviewing their latest unfortunate casualty – but for us to be there in person was quite strange. We were ushered inside by the silent and slowly moving queue forming behind us, and as we passed through the large wooden doorway, we were surprised when we suddenly found ourselves in a busy café. We had expected to be confronted by a reception desk and security staff, but in contrast, we entered into a vibrant environment where suited and robed professionals drank coffee together as they discussed the forthcoming events of the day or sat on comfy sofas reading quality newspapers. At the far end of the room was a counter serving drinks and sandwiches with the opportunity to purchase light snacks if required. We bought ourselves a drink each and sat down at one of the tables, trying to come to terms with our surroundings; it was not at all what we had expected. On either side of the cafe area, there was a wooden door leading into a courtroom with a large meeting room positioned beyond the front wall of the cafe. After finishing our drinks, we retired to the meeting room where we waited for some of the other families to arrive and the introduction to the day's proceedings by the solicitor to begin.

The door of the meeting room opened into a large room with a high ceiling and tall windows. Taking centre stage was an enormous oval table made from a dark wood and surrounded by matching chairs. In the centre of the table, glass jugs full of cold water had been carefully placed, accompanied by drinking glasses. As some of the other families began to arrive in the room and settled themselves around the oval table, Gra and I poured ourselves some water. After waiting a few minutes, the solicitor and other staff from the company entered the room and introduced themselves. Gra and I had been waiting for the inquest to commence since Ben's funeral, for we hoped we would now receive an explanation and reason of how and why Ben was killed.

After the solicitor had concluded the meeting with the families, there was time for a short break before we entered the courtroom and the proceedings began. Our solicitor was present at the front of the court, as was the solicitor representing the Ministry of Defence (MOD). As we all sat down, it soon became apparent just how important it was to have legal representation at an inquest such as this one. Formal discussions between the two legal teams and the Coroner took up most of the morning, and there was a considerable amount of the content and jargon that we didn't understand. However, when all the points had been completed, another pre-inquest meeting was arranged for 29 February. Before the families left for home, the solicitor gathered us together for a question and answer session, at which additional families requested representation by the solicitor.

As we were now familiar with the travelling time and

route to the Oxford Coroner's Court, we decided that for the second pre-inquest meeting we would not travel to Oxford the evening before, but get up early on the morning of the pre-inquest and make the journey there and back on the same day. The second pre-inquest hearing was to operate along the same lines as the first, but with one exception – a buffet lunch had been arranged at a hotel in Oxford where the families would have the opportunity to meet Mr Charles Haddon-Cave QC. He was the QC that had been appointed by the Government on the day of the release of the Board of Inquiry report. He was to head the review ordered by the MOD into the wider aspects relating to the loss of Nimrod XV230.

On the morning of the second pre-inquest hearing, we left home in the early morning so as to arrive in plenty of time for the families' meeting with the legal team, to be held again at the Oxford Coroner's Court. Although I am not a natural early morning person, once I am out of bed and dressed I do appreciate the calm and peacefulness that surrounds the early hours of the day. The meeting was arranged for 9.30am and scheduled to last for an hour, and at 10.30am, the pre-inquest hearing was due to begin, concluding at approximately 12.30pm.

The third pre-inquest hearing was similar to the first two, with some of the discussions in court making sense to us, but other parts not. As the third and final pre-inquest drew to a close, Gra and I could now count the days until the full inquest was due to begin on the 7 May 2008. For the duration of the pre-inquest hearings, Gra continued to gather further information regarding Nimrod XV230 and the rest of the Nimrod fleet from his own investigations and the many supporters that took considerable risks in order to obtain information for us.

As the start date of the inquest drew nearer, there were plenty of matters to be dealt with before departing for Oxford. We would be away from home for the best part of three weeks, probably returning home only briefly for one of the weekends. I had arranged with my place of work to take three weeks off, the length of time the inquest had been scheduled to run for, but had agreed that should the inquest come to an end before the three weeks, then I would return to work. I should add that throughout this whole dreadful experience, from 2 September 2006 to the present day, my employer and work colleagues have always allowed me leave on the many times I have requested in relation to Ben's death, and I sincerely appreciated that. As Gra is self-employed and works from home, his working day allows him more flexibility than mine does and he is able to rearrange his workload to fit around matters of more importance, such as the inquest.

Gra's final task before we left was to take our two dogs to the kennel where they would be staying for the duration of the inquest. Our two sons would also be attending the inquest but only for a few days at the start of it and again for a few days at the conclusion. Matt would be accompanied by his wife, while Andy and his partner would attend whenever their work enabled them to do so. Our accommodation was to be in a hotel on the outskirts of Oxford which was conveniently situated next to a Park & Ride. From there, we could catch a bus that would take us to Oxford city centre, where we could alight directly opposite the Coroner's Court. Although the hotel had many facilities – restaurant, swimming pool, sauna and steam room, and a beauty therapy suite – Gra was satisfied just to have a smoking room and WiFi access. After arriving at the hotel and having taken our suitcases to our rooms, we arranged to go out for a meal together where we could discuss any last minute points that needed clarification before the start of the inquest the following day.

Although the start of the inquest was formerly 6 May

2008, the first day would not be spent in the courtroom. It had been arranged that the families, and those members of the legal teams who wished to do so, would visit RAF Brize Norton where they would be able to view a partially stripped down Nimrod R2 aircraft identical to Nimrod XV230. This would enable those people who were unfamiliar with a Nimrod MR2 to gain a little knowledge regarding the layout of the aircraft and hopefully provide a better understanding of the facts once the inquest in the Coroner's Court began.

We were taken from the Coroner's Court to RAF Brize Norton by coach, and as we entered the neatly-kept grounds where polite people in smart blue uniforms walked, I was very aware of the seriousness of our visit. We were to view the aircraft a few people at a time, and as we did so, RAF personnel would accompany our every move, explaining the different parts of the aircraft to us. As our turn to view the aircraft arrived, we slowly and sombrely climbed the steps into the fuselage of the aircraft. Callum, our first grandchild born three months after Ben was killed, was very well behaved throughout the whole day, and although he will not be able to remember the visit to RAF Brize Norton nor the tour of the Nimrod, I am glad he was there to experience it. I felt spiritually closer to Ben while I was on the aircraft, for that was his place of work. I could picture where he would have sat and understood some of the work he undertook, but I know Gra didn't like being on the aircraft at all and it took all his strength to try and focus only on the technical features and not on Ben. When the visit was complete and the coach had returned us to the Coroner's Court, we made our way back to the hotel, all feeling rather tired and tearful.

Andy and his partner, Deborah, were unable to make the visit Brize Norton but were going to meet us at the Coroner's Court the following day. Although work commitments didn't allow Andy and Matt to attend the inquest every day, they had made arrangements to be there at the start and again for its conclusion, Andy also managed to attend on additional days midway through the inquest which pleased Gra and me.

An RAF liaison officer and four of the other families attending the inquest were provided with accommodation at the same hotel as us. Therefore, a minibus had been arranged to take us all from the hotel to the Coroner's Court in Oxford each morning. As Gra and I boarded the smart minibus for the short journey on the first morning in court, I thought about the much longer journey we had been on since 2 September 2006 and wondered why God had singled us out to be part of such a horrendous experience. As the minibus arrived at the Coroner's Court and the sun shone brightly, we could see the many TV satellite vans parked along the roadside, all preparing to report the day's happenings in court. Across the busy city centre road in the grounds of the court stood journalists and cameramen all waiting for an opportunity to speak with the families and take pictures of them arriving. Once out of the minibus and across the road, Gra and I paused on the court steps to acknowledge the reporters. We thanked them for the help they had given us over the months and years by their continual reporting of Nimrod XV230. We then entered the main court building.

Inside the building, the cafe area was crowded with relatives, legal representatives, company staff, media people, and a sprinkling of RAF personnel in their crisp blue uniforms. Whenever I saw someone wearing an RAF uniform, it always upset me, although I tried not to let it show. Their presence was just another searing reminder that Ben was dead, and that didn't seem fair to me. I wanted to know why God had chosen to take Ben and not one of these other uniformed people. Why my Ben, why not someone else? But I realised I was never going to get that question answered.

The majority of the seating in the cafe area had been taken, leaving only a few empty seats scattered around the room. The tables, if not in a state of disarray from used coffee cups and empty sandwich packaging, served as desks for the many laptops people had brought with them. As I glanced around the room, I caught sight of people that we had not met for quite a while but who we had many communications with via emails and telephone conversations. Whilst waiting for our queue to enter the courtroom, Gra and I spent time in quiet dialogue with them and thanked them for all their help since the loss of XV230.

After about fifteen minutes, the clerk to the court invited those people who were there for the Nimrod inquest into the courtroom. From our attendance at the pre-inquests, we were well aware that seating in the courtroom was harsh. The seating consisted of bare wooden benches with wooden backs providing more than a touch of austerity to the proceedings, and if you didn't want to be crippled with backache by the end of the day, then some type of soft padding was essential. Some people had brought cumbersome cushions to sit on, others laid their coats neatly onto the harsh wood in an attempt to soften their seats, but as the hours and days passed, I found the disagreeable seating triumphed.

Gra and I sat ourselves on the right hand side of the courtroom, just behind the benches where the legal teams were positioned. I had not been in a courtroom before and certainly never attended an inquest so I didn't really know what to expect. After a short wait, the clerk of the court, who was standing at the front of the room behind the Coroner's chair, announced:

All persons having any business before Her Majesty's Assistant Deputy Coroner for

Oxfordshire, particularly in respect of the inquest touching the deaths of the service personnel who lost their lives as a result of the incident involving the Nimrod XV230 in Afghanistan, please draw near and give your attendance.

With that said the Deputy Assistant Coroner for Oxfordshire, Mr Andrew Walker, then entered the court through a door at the front of the room and sat down in his chair. "Thank you very much indeed. Please sit down. I am now going to resume the inquest touching the deaths of..." and he proceeded to read out the fourteen names of those killed aboard Nimrod XV230. He continued addressing the members of the families, explaining that the inquest was similar to an inquiry and that no one was on trial. He said the inquest was a legal requirement in order to confirm four factual questions: who had died, when they died, where they died, and how they came by their deaths. He offered his deepest sympathies to us all, recognizing, however, that there would be nothing that he could ever say to us that would comfort us with our loss. The Coroner then turned to one of the barristers and asked him if he would be kind enough to introduce the parties who appeared before him in court that day.

We were pleased that the Coroner for the inquest was to be Andrew Walker, for he was a very intelligent and knowledgeable man and was not afraid to speak his mind. He had presided over many military inquests, and over recent months, had aggravated the Defence Secretary by some of the words he had chosen to use. On a number of occasions at these inquests, he had used such words as 'serious failings' when referring to the MOD, and like a dripping tap, it had eventually aggravated the Government to such an extent that they had tried, and failed, to ban coroners using this phrase. We were grateful that here was someone who was not going to let the Government bully him into submission.

As the inquest began, Gra and I understood that there would be some upsetting moments. We realized we would have to find strength from within ourselves as we listened for three weeks to Ben's fellow colleagues and experts from companies such as BAE Systems, QinetiQ and Rolls Royce, to name just a few, as they discussed the events surrounding Ben's death. During the first week of the inquest, the court was emptied of all but the families for a short while one morning, as the cockpit recording was played. The recording revealed the first moments when the crew realised there was a fire on board, through to six minutes and six seconds later when the stricken aircraft exploded in the skies above Afghanistan. It was heartbreaking listening to the recording, but certainly something that I felt I had to do.

There had been no problems reported with Nimrod XV230 prior to the aircraft becoming airborne, and one hour and forty-five minutes into the flight, the aircraft rendezvoused with a TriStar Tanker in order for air-to-air refuelling to take place. It was only after air-to-air refuelling had been successfully completed that a bomb bay fire warning was heard on the crew intercom. On the recording, some of the crew could be heard calmly describing smoke coming from the rear bay, and then flames from the rear of the starboard side engine. The crew continued to remain thoroughly professional throughout and responded to the emergency in the manner they had been trained. The pilot began making plans to land at Kandahar, some forty miles away after declaring those most harrowing of words, "MAYDAY, MAYDAY". As they acknowledged the weather at Kandahar airfield, the BOI states: "The crew clearly still believed that they were in control of their aircraft and that they would reach Kandahar." Tragically, that was not to be.

After the recording had finished, we left the courtroom for a short recess, allowing us time to digest the enormity of what we had just heard. Gra and I hugged each other in silence, for there were no words to be found that could possibly offer any comfort at that time. I just hoped, above all else, that Ben firmly believed that they were going to make it to Kandahar airfield and that they would land safely; I find it unbearable to consider the alternative.

Outside the courtroom, the media watched in silent reverence as the families filed out, only imagining what it must have been like for us. Out of respect, they made no attempt to question us. We stood outside on the court steps, and as the sun shone down from a beautiful clear blue sky, office workers and shoppers hurriedly darted between shops and sandwich bars. It was all a stark contrast to what we had just experienced in the courtroom and a sad reminder that life does indeed go on, even though there are times when you do not want it to. Gra and I had not been to Oxford before, and I only wish our first visit had been for a different reason than to attend Ben's inquest. The bright, warm, early summer sunshine seemed to provide an air of well being in the busy city centre. In contrast, I found myself focusing on the fact that Ben would never again feel the warmth of the sun on his young face nor laugh and joke like the young professionals were doing as they moved quickly from work to lunch.

I do not like the phrase 'time heals', for I tend to think that if something is healed then it suggests it is better and back to its original form and life for us can never go back to how it was before Ben died. However, I do realize that I am in a better place now, mentally, than I was during the time of the inquest. But time hasn't healed me; it has just allowed me to grow a little stronger, enabling me to face yet another long year without Ben.

After lunch, we retraced our steps back from the

exuberance of the busy city centre and into the sombre setting of the Oxfordshire Coroner's Court. During the afternoon session, an RAF pathologist took to the stand. He apologised to all the families for any additional distress that may have been caused by DNA complications, which initially led to the wrongful identification of some body parts. We were informed that there were over four hundred body parts collected from the crash site and identification had been a long process. When I eventually received Ben's death certificate, it stated that he had died from multiple injuries. Andrew Walker later added in court: "Whatever role the error played in this case, the distress it caused to the families cannot be quantified."

The most contentious part of the pathologist's evidence was when he said, "On the balance of probabilities, my findings would favour the fuselage being intact and the injuries being caused at the time that that had struck the ground. But I cannot exclude other possibilities."

Gra and I had believed Ben was killed instantly when the aircraft exploded in the sky, but now we were being told that he may have been alive until his body hit the ground, and that was not what we wanted to hear. I didn't want to think of Ben being in pain and frightened as he waited to impact with the ground, and the end of his life.

Further evidence was provided by a Harrier GR7 pilot who was flying a few thousand feet above XV230 and observed the fire and the explosion of the aircraft. His evidence was very graphic and upsetting but he witnessed Ben's final moments before he died, and therefore we listened intently to everything he had to say.

The Coroner asked him if he felt that XV230 was totally destroyed in the explosion in the air and he replied, "Yes, it was totally destroyed before it hit the ground."

After he had finished giving his evidence, Gra caught up with him outside the court and thanked him for his invaluable contribution to the inquest. However, we now had two, quite different, viewpoints on how Ben was killed. The RAF pathologist said, in his opinion, Ben died when the fuselage hit the ground. The Harrier pilot said he was of the opinion that, because the explosion blew the aircraft into many pieces, those on board would have been killed instantly in the explosion. The Coroner did inform us that the difference of opinion, regarding whether Ben died in the explosion in the sky or in the fuselage when it impacted with the ground, could be further examined but it would most likely be upsetting in its detail. Gra and I discussed the issue between us and came to the conclusion that we didn't want to pursue the matter any further. Since the loss of XV230, Gra and I were of the opinion that Ben was killed in the initial explosion in the sky and we continue to hold that belief; the other theory is too upsetting for us to contemplate.

As the days turned into weeks and witness after witness took to the stand, it became clear that the original design and additional modifications had rendered Nimrod XV230 un-airworthy. One witness told how he was shocked by corrosion he had found on fuel pipe couplings on another Nimrod, and when further checks were ordered across the fleet, the problem was widespread. Lengthy discussions on the subject of corrosion then followed.

After three long, uncomfortable weeks listening to how and why Ben died, the final day of the inquest arrived. As a respect to all fourteen men who died aboard Nimrod XV230, a representative from each family laid a red rose on the steps of the court's main entrance. The children of the crew members, who were now all fatherless, each laid a white rose. The press and TV were there in force, some had been there throughout the inquest and others were present at the start and the finish only. Andy, Deborah, Matt and his wife filed into court with us, as Gra and I proceeded to our usual seats for the final time. After a short wait, the Deputy Assistant Coroner, Mr Andrew Walker, entered the Coroner's Court as complete silence descended upon the room.

After his usual welcome and introduction, which after three weeks we were accustomed to, Andrew Walker took approximately thirty minutes to present his narrative verdict as he said, "The crew and passengers were not to know that this aircraft, like every other aircraft within the Nimrod fleet, was not airworthy. What is more, the aircraft was, in my judgment, never airworthy from the first release to service in 1969 to the point where the Nimrod XV 230 was lost." He added that he would report to the Secretary of State that the Nimrod fleet should not fly until the ALARP (as low as reasonably practicable) standards are met. He finished his verdict with the following words:

The fourteen members of crew and passengers of XV230 Nimrod Mk 2 aircraft, which left from an operational base to fly a mission into Afghanistan on 2 September 2006 at 9.13, were lost when shortly after air-to-air refuelling fuel from a fuel leak, most likely from a fuel feed pipe, was ignited by a hot duct within, or closely associated with, dry bay 7 on the starboard side of the aircraft. As there was no fire detection and suppression system within dry bay 7, the crew could do nothing to prevent the fire and the aircraft broke up in the air following an ignition of fuel from fuel tank 7 as the crew were preparing for an emergency landing at Kandahar Airport. Their deaths were in part a result of failures, some of them serious, that resulted in the dangers inherent within dry bay 7

143

of the aircraft created by the introduction of a hot air engine cross feed system and subsequently a bleed from that system on the part of the aircraft manufacturer and those responsible for the safety of the aircraft, going unnoticed. The creation of a baseline safety case in the Cassandra hazard log that contained serious errors failed to deal adequately, or at all, with the danger deposed by dry bay 7 and the danger remained until its discovery after the loss of the aircraft crew and passengers.

It was very, very depressing and dispiriting listening as Andrew Walker read out his damning verdict. It seemed Ben had been killed because he had been flying in an un-airworthy aircraft, and those people charged with the safety of the aircraft failed in their duty. He was killed, not by insurgents, but by incompetence of his own side, the RAF and the MOD, to ensure that the aircraft was airworthy. However, this was not really a surprise for us; our own enquiries had let us to suspect this probable outcome for many months.

When the Coroner had taken his leave, Gra and I slowly abandoned the courtroom for the final time, shuffling past the many legal representatives and the mounds of papers that surrounded them. In the cafe area, the press and TV people were eager to ask us questions and take their photographs. However, advance arrangements had been put in place by our solicitors to use an empty courtroom for a press conference, so we dutifully filed into the room and sat down on wooden benches again. Within minutes of the press conference starting, one of the journalists spoke out, saying he had just been informed of a response from the Armed Forces Minister. Apparently, the MOD had announced they would not ground the entire fleet and believed the aircraft were safe to fly. Andy immediately commented that the statement by the MOD was a disgrace and added, "This plane is not airworthy, it has not been for forty years. It is not airworthy today by the MOD's own regulations and standards and it should not be flying." I was not surprised to hear the statement from the MOD. Ever since the loss of XV230, the RAF and MOD had tried to dismiss the serious problems the Nimrod fleet was experiencing.

Later in the afternoon, on that final day of the inquest, the Armed Forces Minister was interviewed on BBC Radio 4. During the interview, he was asked if the MOD were to blame for the accident, and he answered:

Yes. This aircraft had been flying for many years with a fundamental design fault that just hadn't been recognised and it took this crash in order for it to be recognised.

Since first hearing of Ben's death, I have always felt that Gra was the one bearing the anger. I considered myself in a state of disbelief and extreme sadness, but not anger. However, twelve words, spoken by the Armed Forces Minister on the afternoon of the final day of the inquest, angered me immensely and absolutely disgusted me, and I think will for the rest of my life: "… and it took this crash in order for it to be recognised."

10

The Nimrod Review –
A Failure of Leadership, Culture and Priorities

Mr Haddon-Cave QC was a tall, impeccably dressed, softly spoken man who greeted us all individually as we entered the meeting room within the exclusive Oxford hotel. At the time of the Board of Inquiry release in December 2007, the Secretary of State for Defence had appointed him to explore the wider issues surrounding the loss of Nimrod XV230 and to clarify matters of responsibility. This was our first meeting with him but his gentle manner soon put us at our ease. Prior to the meeting beginning, we were served with refreshments from an array of foods neatly arranged on a table at the rear of the room, together with tea, coffee and soft drinks. Once we had all eaten and were seated with a warm drink, he began to talk in a deep tone and a deliberate manner that over the months we became accustomed to.

He began by informing us briefly of the high profile cases he had been connected with in the past, before beginning to explain his terms of reference for the Nimrod review. He promised that he would leave no stone unturned in assessing where responsibility lay for any failures and what lessons needed to be learned. Gra and I were pleased to have the opportunity to meet with him, and when the afternoon meeting drew to a close, Gra came away confident that those people responsible for the loss of Nimrod XV230 would be brought to justice. Looking back now, we recognise the naivety of our optimism. I was far more dubious, not because of anything Mr Haddon-Cave had said, but because I was always aware that Nimrod had the makings of a political hot potato and was by no means an *independent* tragedy.

As the months passed by, Mr Haddon-Cave kept us informed, usually by letter, of how the investigation was progressing. We were also provided with a direct line telephone number on which to contact him, if at any time we wished to do so. He had an exceptional team of people who worked with him and were at the hub of the investigation. Between them, they collected such a considerable amount of information that storing the paperwork necessitated a separate room, complete with box files literally from floor to ceiling. During the twenty-two months the review took to complete, Mr Haddon-Cave QC arranged a number of meetings with the families, inviting them to meet with him at his London offices to see the progress that was being made. Eventually, the review was complete and preparations were put in place to deliver the findings to Parliament, the families, and the general public.

The week commencing Monday 26 October 2009 was to be the week we had been waiting for since the release of the Board of Inquiry Report on 4 December 2007. To Gra and I, and our other two sons, Andy and Matt, it had seemed a very long wait – almost two years since the Nimrod review began, and just over three years since the loss of Nimrod XV230 over Afghanistan and the devastating death of Ben. As the review slowly progressed, there had been much speculation as to what the completed article may or may not contain. Again, Gra was optimistic and I was not.

At mid-day on Wednesday 28 October, we would hear where fault lay for Ben's death. It had certainly been a long and painful wait. Since the crash of XV230, we had been trying to uncover as many of the facts as possible surrounding the loss of the aircraft. Many people had been helping us in this task, good people who we didn't know of before the crash, one even from abroad. However, there had also been people who were less supportive of our quest for the truth. I considered them to be mainly people who had served a long career in the RAF. As is often the case, they looked back on those times with happy and nostalgic memories, but I felt their nostalgia blinded them to the present day airworthiness issues that were a real threat to safety. I think they found it difficult to accept that the RAF may have been responsible for such a tragic accident and immense loss of life. Their comments had hurt me greatly at a time when I was still grieving so painfully for Ben, but Gra was stoic throughout and coaxed me gently through those bad times. There was never any doubt in our minds that we had to continue on this sad journey in search of the true facts, for the sake of Ben.

On Sunday evening, 25 October, we had received a telephone call from one of the other families whose loved one was killed when XV230 crashed. She asked whether we had received any media interest regarding the forthcoming release of the review and we said it had been unusually quiet. But that was shortly to change. On Monday morning, a couple of newspaper reporters had made contact with us by telephone and we also heard from two television companies. The TV people asked if they could visit us at home to record interviews with us before we travelled up to London on the Tuesday afternoon. Gra agreed that a reporter from the Press Association and the BBC could come and interview us on Tuesday morning.

I don't usually like talking to TV cameras as I detest my Midlands accent, although, thankfully many people seem to confuse it with a more northern accent. I had taken part in media interviews in the past, but generally I am not relaxed doing them, and therefore do not put myself forward willingly. However, as I pondered over the booked interviews for Tuesday morning, I found I did not possess the usual panic; in fact, I actually wanted to be a part of the interviews. I felt ready to announce to the country the great pain and injustice we had suffered by Ben's sudden and unexpected death and the subsequent secretive nature of the MOD and the RAF as we endeavoured to uncover all the facts relating to the loss of XV230. Many more media people contacted us during the Monday afternoon, and the day seemed to be taken up by answering telephone calls and packing clothes for Tuesday's long awaited journey to London.

By the time Tuesday morning arrived, all the return phone calls had been made, a small suitcase had been packed for an overnight stay in London, and the house had been tidied. Whenever I go away from home for a period of time, I always feel the need to leave the house in a state of tidiness. If anyone needed to enter the house while we were away, at least it would be tidy and clean; but why anyone would be entering the house legitimately in our absence didn't make any sense. But just in case they did, then the house would not let me down. I knew it was my neurosis surfacing, but I was comfortable with it and I was too old and tired to fight it. Gra had arranged to take our two dogs to the kennels at 2.00pm, which left us just enough time to get to the station to catch the train.

As we waited for the television people to arrive, I found myself eager to talk with them. I knew what information they wanted from us; they wanted to know what we hoped to hear from Charles Haddon-Cave's twenty-two month review. Without hesitation, I knew what I wanted to hear; I wanted to know who was responsible for killing Ben and what action would be taken against them. I also wanted to meet with those accused so I could try and explain to them the devastation they had caused our family, but I was soon to learn that it was not going to be that straightforward.

The first interviewer and cameraman arrived on time,

which was a good start, as schedules were going to be very tight throughout the day and there would be no room for unpunctuality by anyone. On the few occasions I have spoken on camera, the interviewer usually likes Gra and myself seated next to each other on the settee, but that day, I didn't want or need that. I was so fervent that I was prepared to do the interview on my own; in fact, I preferred to do it on my own. Gra could talk to them afterwards if he still wanted to. This new confidence I seemed to possess that morning was born out of a very long wait for answers regarding who was responsible for Ben's death. I believed this to be the end of the road. We still had on going court action in process, but that just plods wearily on at its own monotonous pace, year in and year out. The Nimrod review, however, was to be the end of the investigative work; everything there was to find out about Nimrod and airworthiness should now have been uncovered. And so, to the amazement of Gra, I did the first interview on my own and was happy for the second interview to follow along the same lines, which it did. Eventually, after a very busy morning and with all the cameras gone and the dogs safely in the kennels, we were on our way to London, hopefully to find out who killed Ben and why it was allowed to happen.

Sky News had arranged for someone to meet us at Waterloo Station. A driver was to collect us from the station and take us to the Sky studio where Gra would record an interview for them. The subject of the interview, being similar to the interviews done the previous day at home by me, was – what were we hoping to hear at Wednesday's review?

As the train rattled towards its destination, from rural Somerset to urbanised London, Gra and I sat quietly amongst the crowded carriage. None of the other passengers knew how important this journey was to us, we were all linked by the same journey and heading in the same direction but with totally different expectations and outcomes. Students listened to their iPods and businessmen read their newspapers as Gra and I sat in silence, contemplating how long and harrowing our journey had been since we first heard the devastating news of the loss of a Nimrod aircraft on 2 September 2006. The events of that day had totally transformed our lives, and the last three years had been stressful and tormenting as we tried to come to terms with Ben's death, at the same time delving into the murky corridors of the MOD in our search of answers.

By the time we arrived at Waterloo Station, it was already dark outside, and while we were just arriving, many more people were departing. Once we were out of the station boundaries, Gra immediately lit himself a cigarette, the first one he had had since leaving the uniformly green fields of Somerset two and a half hours earlier. The driver and car that was to meet us at the station had already been described to us in a previous telephone conversation so locating them was not a problem.

As soon as Gra had finished his cigarette, we climbed into the smart white waiting car and were driven to the television studios. Although we now lived in Somerset, we were not strangers to London. Gra and I had both visited the city on many occasions as children and teenagers, and since Ben's death, solicitors and the Nimrod review had necessitated we visit on many occasions. Our choice of travel in London had always been by taxi, rather than bus or tube. With a taxi, we didn't need to struggle to plan a route, all we needed to do was put an arm out and a taxi would stop and take us to whichever destination we required. We also considered the fares to be very reasonable indeed.

Once inside the studios, I was surprised to recognise faces I had only before seen on our television at home, which amused Gra. A young man approached us and introduced himself before beginning to explain his expectations for the interview. It was agreed that I would do the first interview on my own that evening and Gra would return to the studios early the following morning to do his interview. The arrangement seemed ideally tailored around us, as I do not like rising too early in the morning and Gra is usually awake and out of bed by 6.30am. However, his interview was later cancelled and replaced by another news item, something that we had both become accustomed to over the years in the news business. We had learnt that news is very transient, important one moment only to be replaced by something considered even more important the next.

I was led through to a rather unglamorous room that held an assorted collection of items you might have expected to find forgotten in a storeroom. One of the items was a tall wooden stool, which the young man pointed to at the same time as telling me to sit down. I did as I was told and perched myself uncomfortably on the edge of the stool. A mobile bookcase was wheeled into position behind me and a photographer sat in front of me. The interviewer stood off screen and was only present by his voice. He asked me similar questions to those I had previously been asked by the other reporters, relating mainly to what I hoped to hear from Wednesday's review. Again, I gave the same reply that I had given on so many occasions lately, that I was hoping to find out who was responsible for killing Ben and what action had been or would be taken against them. The interview was short but to the point, and I was satisfied with how it developed. When the required questions had been asked of me, I awkwardly climbed down from the stool, and Gra and I returned through the room of recognisable faces and out into the darkness of a warm October night. The same driver and car were waiting outside the studios for us and whisked us away to our hotel, somewhere in the maze that is central London.

I had expected to have difficulty sleeping that night, with

the importance of the following day playing on my mind. However, all the travelling and many interviews of the last few days outweighed my nervousness and I fell sound asleep within seconds of my head touching the hotel pillow.

The following day, Wednesday 28 October 2009, I awoke at 7.30am. The weather was dry, sunny and very mild for the time of year. Gra was already awake and dressed so I washed and dressed quickly and we descended the tired staircase to breakfast, wondering what the day had in store for us. Although we'd had a number of television and radio stations requesting to interview us that morning, we had declined. We had not wanted to begin the day feeling rushed; we wanted to take our time and be alone with our thoughts. It was an important day, we had waited twenty-two months to hear what was going to be said today and we felt it deserved some respect. There would be plenty of time for interviews afterwards.

By 10.00am, we were ready to leave the hotel and make our way by taxi to Quadrant Chambers, where the review findings were going to be explained to us by Mr Haddon-Cave QC. One of the things Gra and I liked about London was the fact that you can hail a taxi from wherever you are. You don't need to suffer an unspecified wait for a bus which will take you to an anonymous place en route, nor struggle with a life size map which always refuses to return to its original pocket size. The black cabs dart around the London streets like ants in a nest, always busy and always on the move. A taxi will usually appear within a couple of minutes of waiting and take you to your destination quickly and at a very reasonable cost.

As we climbed into the taxi that was to take us to Chambers, Gra unsurprisingly received a telephone call from Radio 4 and proceeded to do an interview with them as we travelled across London in the rear of a black cab. As the taxi drew up at our destination, Gra's interview came to an end. I paid the fare and we alighted into the vibrant streets of London. Once outside of the taxi, Gra received another telephone call from a reporter and proceeded to engage in conversation with him. As I stood alone in the crowded street, waiting for the call to come to an end, I was surprised to see a TV cameraman and a reporter outside Chambers. The exact whereabouts of the review meeting had not been disclosed to the media so as to avoid any press intrusion to the families. The reporter walked towards me and asked me if I was someone else; I said I wasn't, but didn't say who I was, and the disappointed reporter retraced his steps back to the cameraman. Gra was still engaged in conversation with the reporter on the other end of his phone whilst smoking a final cigarette before the review.

When he had finished with both the reporter and the cigarette, we made our way into Chambers, by which time the other families were also beginning to arrive. Once inside the building, we proceeded to the reception desk where a confident lady took our coats and handed us each a name badge. We were then ushered through to the library, where rows of chairs had been dutifully arranged for us and books from past years lined the walls. At the rear of the library, on neatly arranged tables, lay the customary array of cups and saucers, accompanied by jugs of tea and coffee. As we awaited the arrival of Mr Haddon-Cave, we mingled with some of the other families, exchanging pleasantries and sipping hot drinks. When all the families that were expected had eventually arrived, Mr Haddon-Cave entered the room, and as the door closed behind him, a hush of expectation descended upon the old library.

Charles Haddon-Cave QC began by welcoming everyone to the Chambers and acknowledged that the day was a very important one for all of us. He explained briefly why the review had taken so long to complete, but assured us that no stone had been left unturned in his pursuit for the facts surrounding the loss of Nimrod XV230 and general airworthiness within the RAF. Once the Secretary of State for Defence had read out a summary of the report at the House of Commons, Mr Haddon-Cave said he would need to attend a press conference a short distance away from Chambers. He added that a closed circuit live feed would be relayed back to the families waiting in the library. Copies of *The Nimrod Review* were then wheeled into the library through the door at the side and everyone in the room was presented with a copy.

The full title of the report was *The Nimrod Review: An independent review into the broader issues surrounding the loss of the RAF Nimrod MR2 Aircraft XV230 in Afghanistan in 2006.* The *Review* consisted of 586 pages, was three and a quarter centimetres thick, and weighed two and a half kilograms. Mr Haddon-Cave talked us through the most significant parts of the *Review* and directed us to specific areas of interest and importance. As we looked through the pages, we realised that Charles Haddon-Cave and his team had certainly done a thorough and lengthy job, but at the same time, I found myself feeling angry and upset; angry at the magnitude of the failings within the RAF and MOD that were highlighted, and that for the three years since the loss of XV230, the RAF and MOD had been telling us there was nothing really wrong with XV230, and that it was just a 'tragic accident'. Now, with the *Review* in front of us, we could see that it was in fact an accident waiting to happen, and it was just a matter of *when* not *if*. Ben just happened to be in the wrong place at the wrong time!

My eyes filled with tears as, yet again, I realised that Ben need not have died; if only those people whose job it was to ensure airworthiness had done what they were paid to do, Ben could still have been alive today. Looking at the situation logically, I wondered to myself what Ben's reaction would have been if he had been able to listen to what Mr Haddon-Cave was saying to us that day. I have heard it said that once you are dead you bear no anger, but if someone had asked Ben while he was alive whether he wanted to remain alive or take a ride in an aircraft that would kill him, I am sure he would have chosen to remain alive. One can deduce, therefore, that he would have been cross when he realised someone had killed him.

When Mr Haddon-Cave had finished talking to the families, he was driven to another building where he read his seven page statement to the waiting media. A copy of the statement had also been distributed to the families. This was to enable us to follow what was said as Mr Haddon-Cave read his copy out aloud to the many journalists that had gathered together that day, eagerly awaiting the disagreeable truth. On his arrival at the building where the press were gathered, the closed circuit live feed was switched on and we watched in silence. Mr Haddon-Cave stood upright behind a plain desk and untied the silk bow around the file he held; he then began to read the statement. He began by explaining that he had been appointed by the Secretary of State for Defence, back in December 2007, to determine accountability for any failures and to see what lessons might be learned for future reference. This was followed by a short concise paragraph detailing the sad events of 2 September 2006, the day on which Nimrod XV230 was lost, together with all fourteen servicemen on board – one of them being our much-loved son, Ben. The incident represented the single biggest loss of life of British service personnel since the Falklands War in 1982, when Ben was just fifteen months-old.

The statement, read so eloquently by Mr Haddon-Cave, contained considerable criticism directed at BAE Systems, the RAF, IPT, and QinetiQ. The report 'specifically name[d] and criticise[d] ten individuals for their roles; five from the MOD, three from BAE Systems and two from QinetiQ'. Within the statement, there was a section entitled 'Lessons and Recommendations', in which it was stated that 'the shortcomings in the current airworthiness system in the MOD are manifold'. The final paragraph of the statement began by stating, 'Tragically, for the crew of XV230, the lessons have come too late, and at an infinite price'. However, the section of the statement that I found so dreadfully sad was paragraph five, where the following was stated:

My report concludes that the accident to XV230 was avoidable, and that XV230 was lost because of a systemic breach of the Military Covenant brought about by significant failures on the part of the MOD, BAE Systems and QinetiQ. This must not be allowed to happen again.

Mr Haddon-Cave concluded his reading of the statement and, without allowing any time for questions from the baying press, left the building and returned to the families waiting in the library at Chambers. Back in the library, Gra and I were immersed in *The Nimrod Review*, flicking through the pages that were shaded in blue. One of Mr Haddon-Cave's team told us on which page the names of those who Mr Haddon-Cave considered to hold some responsibility for the loss of XV230 could be found. We quickly turned the pages until we arrived at the names. This is what we had wanted, the names of those people whom he considered, between them, held responsibility for Ben's death. If they had done their jobs properly, Ben may still have been alive today.

When Mr Haddon-Cave arrived back at Chambers, he returned to the library and the many questions that were waiting to be asked of him. However, it had been arranged in advance that the families would meet with the Armed Forces Minister at 3.00pm at the Ministry of Defence, and as taxis had been arranged to take us there, it did not allow us a great deal of time with Mr Haddon-Cave.

As it was nearing 3.00pm, Gra decided to excuse himself from the library in order to have a quick cigarette before we all left for the appointment at the Ministry of Defence. While he was outside, someone suddenly announced that the taxis had arrived and were waiting to take us to the MOD building. Some of the relatives had heard that there were large numbers of press and TV cameras outside the front entrance, so Mr Haddon-Cave hastily arranged an alternative way out of the building for those families that did not want to be confronted by the press. The stark reality that Ben need not have died sent confusion and pain searing through my head, turning to anger as it travelled relentlessly through my veins until it encompassed my whole being. I was so cross and upset by what the *Review* had revealed that I didn't mind talking to the press; in fact, I wanted to talk to them.

I collected my jacket from the cloakroom and marched towards the main entrance of the building. I had not considered the amount of media coverage there would be waiting outside; I was just so pre-occupied with the fact that Ben need not have died that nothing else really registered with me. As I opened the door and stepped out onto the pavement, a swarm of reporters and cameras suddenly surrounded me, all calling to me and wanting to know what my reaction to the *Review* was. Of course, I was just what they wanted – an angry and upset mother. I fought back the tears as I told them it was an absolute disgrace what Mr Haddon-Cave and his team had uncovered, that the Review highlighted everything we had been saying for the past three years, and more. I was so cross – for three years we had been voicing our concerns over failings within the airworthiness process and XV230, and each time, the RAF and MOD had told us we were wrong and that everything was fine with these aircraft.

I was determined not to cry on national television, but that afternoon, I came very close to it. I had a point to get across, that Ben's death was avoidable, and I owed it to Ben to keep in control of the situation. There would be time for personal tears later when we were back in our hotel room alone.

Microphones where being thrust towards my face as the media jostled for the best position, all of them calling out my name. I suddenly wondered where Gra was, hoping he would soon reappear and that his presence would attract the majority of the press in his direction, releasing some of the pressure from me. As I quickly turned my head and looked to the right of me, I saw him, standing alone and being interviewed by a lady from the BBC. I didn't understand why he only had one reporter with him whilst I was surrounded by the remainder, but I suppose they wanted to know whether I felt I had had my questions answered by the contents of the *Review*. I stood alone, surrounded by cameras and reporters, and answered questions from the media for about fifteen minutes. I was then ushered towards a waiting taxi, which was to drive us to the Ministry of Defence and our meeting with the Armed Forces Minister. A young lady from ITV seemed to be ushering people towards the waiting taxis. Why she took it upon herself to chaperone us that afternoon and evening, I don't know, but she was very helpful and I don't know how we would have managed without her. She ended up staying with us until 9.30pm, when we had returned from the MOD and finally finished all our interviews.

We arrived at the steps of the MOD at about 3.10pm, and although the majority of the families had already arrived, there were still a few families emerging from taxis at the same time as us. As the taxi drew away, it exposed us to more reporters and cameras, all waiting for an opportunity to speak to the families. However, at this location, as opposed to outside Chambers, the police were present on the steps of the MOD entrance and a far more organised gathering prevailed. Gra acknowledged the reporters, informing them that he would speak with them in some length when the meeting with the Armed Forces Minister had ended. We then hurried up the cold, white steps into the spacious building that was the Ministry of Defence.

Once all the security procedures had been adhered to, we were escorted to the meeting room where the Armed Forces Minister had already begun talking to the other families. I found a spare seat at the back of the room and sat down, but I quickly realised I was wasting my time there. It was clear to me that the Armed Forces Minister was there to appease the families, and in my opinion, his words sounded very hollow. I decided my time was too valuable to spend it listening to a feeble explanation by a Government official as to why my child was allowed to fly in an un-airworthy aircraft. I could be reading *The Nimrod Review* in more detail or conveying my disgust to the waiting press.

I whispered to Gra and told him about my plan to leave the room. Then, as suddenly as I had entered the meeting room, I rose from my seat and left, followed by one of the other family members. The two of us were escorted back to the ground floor of the MOD building where some of the staff seemed bewildered that we were leaving after so little time there. But when they realised that I was committed to my intentions, they arranged for a taxi to collect us from the front of the building and return us back to the relative tranquillity of Quadrant Chambers.

As soon as we arrived back at Chambers, I began returning as many of the missed telephone calls on my mobile as I could. However, as I continued to receive incoming calls from the press and television at the same time as I was making outgoing calls, I didn't succeed in replying to them all. Holding my phone to my ear with one hand, I struggled to recover a scrap of paper from the bottom of my handbag with the other, at the same time attempting to scribble legible names and meeting times on the scrap of paper that was much too small for what was required of it. I do know I didn't manage to return all of the calls that day.

Gra returned to Chambers about thirty minutes later; he had walked out of the meeting following an answer from the Armed Forces Minister. Gra had asked the following question: "Now that some of the people responsible for airworthiness had been discredited, how do you know the Nimrod is safe to fly?" The Minister replied, saying that he had asked Mr Haddon-Cave QC if they were safe to fly and he said they were. Gra then added, with respect, that he did not think a QC was appropriately qualified to decide the airworthiness of all Nimrod aircraft and he didn't find that sort of answer reassuring, and with that, he walked out. The other families returned from the meeting at the Ministry of Defence about half an hour after Gra did. We all took our seats in the library again for another meeting with Mr Haddon-Cave as he continued to explain the content of the *Review* to us. Although the meeting continued late into the afternoon, Gra and I left at 4.45pm, before it had come to an end. We had promised to do some interviews with a number of television stations for their evening news programmes, and as the hours were racing by, we really needed to be on our way to the studios. A few of the other families also left early as they had flights to catch home.

Some of the television interviews were recorded live in a studio, others were conducted on College Green opposite the House of Commons, but all wanted the same question answered: What was our response to the Haddon-Cave Review?

There is nothing glamorous about television interviews, they are very monotonous, time consuming, and staged beyond belief. However, the media had been very good to us and remained loyal to our cause from the very beginning of this living nightmare, which began for us some years ago on 2 September 2006. During the very first week of our nightmare, it was apparent to us that Gra and I alone were not going to achieve our objective of finding out who was responsible for Ben's death and bringing them to justice. We realised immediately that we would need help, and a great deal of that help came from the media. They had assisted us on so many occasions by exposing to the public the many failings within the RAF and MOD, that it was only fair that we reciprocate their help by participating with them now.

So the interviews on College Green continued all evening, with the anonymous young lady from ITV still orchestrating the whole sequence of events for us. The final interview took place at 9.30pm, by which time we were both tired and hungry. Neither of us had eaten anything since lunchtime so we went with one of the other relatives to the Strand Hotel for a quiet evening meal and a welcome sit down.

We arrived back at our hotel about 11.00pm, and as I sat on my bed, I slowly and hesitantly began to realise that this was not going to be the end and that this day had opened up even more lines of investigation. Looking back on the day's events, it had been a day of very mixed emotions. Charles Haddon-Cave QC and his team had done a thorough job and we were pleased with the findings exposed in the *Review*. But there was also a feeling of sadness for Ben and the crew, for they had believed the aircraft to be airworthy on that Saturday morning of 2 September 2006 and now the world officially knew that sadly it was not.

The Nimrod Review recommended the establishment of a new independent Military Airworthiness Authority

(MAA) and Regulator to govern all aspects of military aviation. This would be the legacy of the crew of XV230. Hopefully, never again would crews fly in un-airworthy aircraft.

11

Accountability

Gra was bought up in a family where religion and justice were part of normal everyday life. His Grandfather was a magistrate and a Methodist lay preacher, his father was also a Methodist lay preacher, and his brother was a magistrate, so honesty and justice has featured strongly throughout his life.

A few months after Ben was killed, it quickly became apparent that, although his death was accidental as opposed to a deliberate act, there were people who were responsible. Had they done things differently and perhaps more precisely, the subsequent outcome of fourteen deaths may have been avoided. Indeed, Charles Haddon-Cave QC stated as much in *The Nimrod Review*, which he was appointed to conduct. He writes:

> *My Report concludes that the accident to XV230 was avoidable, and that XV230 was lost because of a systemic breach of the Military Covenant brought about by significant failures on the part of the MOD, BAE System, and QinetiQ.*

Following the release of the Board of Inquiry findings, together with the considerable amount of information people had passed to Gra, it certainly did seem to us that there were people who held part responsibility for the loss of XV230. It, therefore, seemed only right to us that those people should be held accountable for their actions and for justice to be done, although at the time we were not sure how to pursue this.

However, one morning, quite unexpectedly, Gra received a telephone call from a lady whose relative had been amongst those killed in an incident in Iraq. This tragic event had seen a British Hercules shot down by Iraqi insurgents using small arms fire, with the loss of all servicemen on board. Gra had spoken with her before but her latest telephone call was quite different to previous calls. In Wiltshire, the inquest of the servicemen killed in the incident was taking place and she said the barrister representing some of the families would be interested in talking with Gra. At the time, and this was before the release of *The Nimrod Review*, Gra and I considered Nimrod XV230 un-airworthy and it had been suggested to us that the incident in Iraq may also have been caused by an aircraft being un-airworthy.

A few days later, Gra travelled to Wiltshire to meet the barrister. The journey is about an hour's drive from where we live in Somerset, and although in miles the distance is not great, the route is very rural and consists mainly of meandering B-roads. However, it was the beginning of spring, and as the weather was dry and bright, Gra said his journey was a pleasant one. The inquest was being held at Trowbridge Town Hall, an impressive looking building that was presented to the residents of the town by a local businessman in 1889 to celebrate Queen Victoria's fiftieth year on the throne. One of the many functions currently accommodated in the building is that of inquests and military inquests.

As Gra walked through the main doors of the building, he was suddenly confronted by four police officers in stab jackets. One of them asked if they could help him, and when Gra replied by telling them he was there for the current inquest, they wanted to know why the inquest was of interest to him. He told them that he'd been invited to attend that day by one of the barristers involved and they immediately asked him his name. When he replied "Graham Knight", they said, "Yes, you are expected" and let him in. Gra was rather taken aback by the manner of the four police officers; after all, the inquest was open to the public and he had certainly not expected such an abrupt reception. He understood that at times sensitive information was being heard in-camera, but he felt the level of security that day was somewhat intimidating, especially during an *open* session.

He slipped quietly into the room where the inquest was taking place and found himself a vacant seat; he sat down and listened intently to the proceedings until the Coroner announced it was time for a short break.

During the break, he was introduced to the barrister who had invited him there and took an instant liking to him, which is not at all like Gra. Usually, he would reserve his judgment until a further meeting with the person, but he said there was something about this man that made him think *I can trust this guy*, adding that he could see the passion in his eyes and feel his energy as he spoke to him about Nimrod. After they had finished their conversation and as Gra got up to leave, the barrister added, "If you ever need me, just give me a ring." Gra said afterwards that he knew they would meet again.

One of the other Nimrod families had continued to ask Gra if any action could be taken in respect of the loss of Nimrod XV230 and the crew, and he decided to ask the barrister he had met at Trowbridge for advice. Gra contacted the barrister and it was agreed that Gra and I would meet with him and a colleague of his early one evening in a quiet pub on the outskirts of Trowbridge. During our journey to meet with them, I was slightly apprehensive, wondering whether this person was going to fully understand our situation and our intentions; but as Gra had spoken so highly of him, I was also looking forward to our meeting. However, I need not have worried, for shortly after we met, I understood why Gra had been willing to put his faith in this person for I too could see the passion this man had for justice and fairness. I was also pleasantly surprised by how knowledgeable he was regarding Nimrod and our progress so far.

As our meeting drew to a close, the barrister said he would contact a firm of solicitors over the following few days regarding a possible case against the MOD. This was in April 2008, and if any court action was to be taken, then paperwork needed to be submitted within two years of the incident, which meant we only had five months remaining. On our return journey home from that evening meeting, Gra and I talked incessantly about what we had discussed in the pub and our liking for the barrister. We felt we had found someone who held similar beliefs to us regarding the Nimrod case, and we didn't feel so alone in what had at times seemed to us a solitary search for justice. Gra certainly felt uplifted; for the first time since the loss of Nimrod XV230 and its crew, he began to see a way forward in his quest to obtain some justice against those people responsible for Ben's death.

The barrister was true to his word, as one would expect, and arranged for us to meet with a solicitors firm in London. Gra and I decided we would travel to London by train instead of going by car. That way we didn't need to concern ourselves with parking, we would simply leave the train in London and hail a taxi. When the day of our meeting arrived, we got up early and drove through the rural tranquillity that is Somerset to the almost deserted railway station on the outskirts of Yeovil. There we caught the early morning train to London.

As the train rattled into Yeovil Junction, we could glimpse through the slowly passing windows to see how empty the carriages were as it gradually came to a halt outside the quaint station cafe. The number of people already waiting at the station to board the train could be counted on one hand. There was a suited man with the customary briefcase and black umbrella, juggling a newspaper and a take-a-way coffee as he endeavoured to control all four items with only two hands. Then there was a respectable looking couple, probably in their early sixties, who I imagined to be embarking on a day trip to the capital. They were both wearing matching waterproof jackets, most likely purchased from a camping shop, and the man carried a 1950s style shopping bag; but they looked content. The only other waiting passenger was a young lad, probably about nineteen or twenty, who looked like a student with decent attire but worn shabbily and, of course, earphones in each ear.

The six of us climbed onto the now stationary train with the elderly couple and myself taking extra care not to fall down the gap between the platform and the train. After a few minutes wait, and with the realisation that no one else was interested in boarding the train so early in the morning, the big hand of the blue station clock gave one more *click* and the journey began. As we travelled sleepily towards our destination through fields and past byroads, each station we stopped at saw more passengers climb aboard until eventually the train appeared full to capacity. The quiet deserted train that we left Somerset on a few hours earlier had arrived in London crammed with people clamouring to escape into the busy streets of the city.

As soon as we were out of the station confines, Gra lit himself a cigarette, the first one he had been able to smoke since leaving Yeovil Junction. A few minutes later, and with his addiction replenished, we hailed a taxi, climbed inside and were on our way to the solicitor's office. Since Ben's death, we had made many journeys to London to visit various people and organizations and found the easiest way for us to travel around London was by taxi. We were not overly familiar with some of the districts and road names, nor did we know which buses would take us to where we wanted to go, therefore, taking a taxi seemed to be the best option for us. We arrived at the solicitor's office about ten minutes early, which was just enough time for Gra to indulge himself in another cigarette before we entered the building.

Once we had presented ourselves at the reception desk, we were ushered into a shiny narrow lift with instructions to press button number three. As the lift came to a halt on the third floor and the doors slid open, I was relieved to be out of it and standing on a more solid surface. I'm claustrophobic. I don't *do* lifts, unless there are no stairs and I really have no choice because I have to be on a certain floor. We followed the directions given to us at reception and found ourselves in a large, brightly lit, open-plan office. A smartly dressed man greeted us and directed us forward into a large room where a sizeable oblong table ran the length of it. Chairs were arranged neatly around the table with a large silver tray containing cups, saucers, milk, tea, coffee, two large flasks of hot water, and a plate of biscuits placed in the centre.

Gra and I sat down, and a few moments later, three people from the company entered the room and introduced themselves. As they began to speak, we were surprised yet pleased by their level of knowledge of Nimrod XV230, but they added that the case had attracted much media coverage over the past two years. As most people will know, employing a solicitor and taking legal action can be very expensive, but we were determined to go ahead with the action if funding could be arranged. The solicitor said that due to the level of public interest in the Nimrod case, and given the facts from the Board of Inquiry and the inquest, they felt that arranging funding for the case would not be a problem. We all sat talking in the room for a couple of hours, and by the time we were ready to leave, Gra felt confident with how the conversation had developed; I was always a little more reserved with my feelings and thoughts.

Over the following months, we visited the solicitors in London on a number of occasions. Sometimes we were accompanied by one of the other families, other times we went alone, with each visit building on the previous one. Any legal action needed to be submitted before the second anniversary of Ben's death, so the paperwork was prepared and lodged with the appropriate body. The solicitors released to the media a statement summarising the legal proceedings that were to be submitted. We would be considering suing the Government under breach of Article 2 of the European Convention on Human Rights. This attracted the interest of television and newspaper journalists who contacted us requesting interviews. As the second anniversary of Ben's death was nearly upon us, the media were also interested to know if we had anything planned for the 2nd of September.

Although there was no automatic monetary award attached to an Article 2 case, a few people still assumed money was the motivation behind our legal challenge. We found these comments hurtful at the time, but I think any parent whose child has been killed will understand our need for accountability. At the time, which was before the Nimrod review had been completed, there were still many people who found it hard to believe that the RAF and MOD could be at fault. However, in October 2009, with the release of *The Nimrod Review: A Failure of Leadership, Culture and Priorities*, people did have to accept the sad fact that the loss of Nimrod XV230 and all fourteen servicemen on board was the result of failures within the MOD, the RAF, and its main contractors.

Once the initial paperwork had been lodged with the court, we then had a further couple of months to finalize the claim details before the final submission of the completed case. The solicitors in London proceeded with what needed to be done at their end, and when all the necessary documents were prepared, the completed paperwork was submitted to the court. The writ was served against the MOD on 23 December 2008 for:

> ... *damages for breach of statutory duty; and declaratory relief that the defendant is in breach of Article 2 of the European Convention of Human Rights. Initially, the case was brought by me as Executrix of the Estate of Benjamin James Knight (deceased) and on her own behalf.*

One of the other families also joined us in this action, and some months later, more families also asked to be included. As was usual for us now, the newspapers and television companies were interested in what we were trying to do, and Gra and I have always appreciated the help and support they have given us over the years. We believed that if we were successful, it could pave the way for other families to bring action against the MOD over the death of loved ones in Iraq or Afghanistan, depending on the situation.

Our solicitors and the MOD legal team attended a number of meetings with the Master – the judge who takes care of provisional hearings at court – and in January 2009, we received copies of the defence papers submitted to the court by the MOD. Within their response, the MOD had stated:

> *It is admitted that the defendant owed to the deceased a Duty of Care and that the accident was caused by a breach of that Duty of Care.*

Although Gra and I had always thought this to be the

171

case, we were very surprised by this unexpected declaration from the MOD. We had expected the MOD to continue to deny any wrongdoing and fight the case all the way to court, but instead they were admitting their guilt. However, we were still a very long way off from getting the case to court and were soon to realise that all the effort and time we had channelled into the legal side was eventually to come to no avail.

A few days before Christmas 2009, a further meeting was held between our solicitors and barrister, the MOD legal team, and the Master in charge of the case. At this meeting, it was announced that if we wished to proceed with the case, we had to do so in the Scottish Courts. We were informed that this was because some of the other families, who joined us in bringing the action, were still in legal proceedings for compensation in the Scottish Courts. However, two months before we received that decision, the law in Scotland had been amended which meant we were not able to continue the case in Scotland as we were out of time. Initially, the outcome was disappointing, but not unexpected. In our efforts to get some justice for Ben, we had come across many obstacles, some could be overcome, others could not. It was just the way it was.

12

The Civil Police Investigation

The details released in *The Nimrod Review* by Charles Haddon-Cave QC on 28 October 2009 reverberated throughout the military aviation world. It was one of the most damning official reports ever published. His findings were scathing, and he named ten people across three organisations – the MOD, BAE Systems, and QinetiQ – all of whom, in his opinion, had failed in their responsibilities to such an extent that he felt they should be publicly named. "I have only named and criticised organisations and individuals where, in my view, it is necessary, fair, proportionate and in the public interest to do so."

In light of the revelations made in the *Review*, our barrister considered that there may be sufficient evidence for charges to be brought against some or all of those individuals and companies named as having some responsibility for the crash. With this fact in mind, he wrote to the Crown Prosecution Service (CPS) on our behalf, enquiring whether there might be sufficient grounds for a criminal investigation to take place. A couple of weeks later, the CPS replied by letter stating that if we considered a criminal offence had been committed, we should report it to our local police so that the appropriate course of action could be taken. Gra therefore collected together what he felt to be all the appropriate paperwork, accompanied with a two-page typed letter, and went along to our local police station to report what, in our opinion, we considered to be a crime – either corporate manslaughter and/or gross negligence manslaughter – committed by the individuals and companies named in *The Nimrod Review*, with the exception of the two serving RAF officers who would come under the remit of the military police

Not surprisingly, the young policeman behind the reception desk at our local police station appeared quite bewildered when he had listened to what Gra had to say and didn't understand why we were reporting this very out of the ordinary situation to him. Gra explained that our barrister had written to the CPS and had been informed that the matter would have to be reported to the police first, which was exactly what he was doing. The policeman then asked him to wait while he went to another room to speak to his sergeant. This was the start of a number of discussions that took place between him and his sergeant until, eventually, they decided to phone Taunton Police Station and speak to a Detective Chief Inspector. The DCI said if Gra took all the information he had with him along to Taunton Police Station, he would have a look through it.

As Christmas was only a few days away, we decided to wait until the New Year before taking the paperwork to Taunton and attempting to explain the rather complicated situation again. However, a few days after Christmas the doorbell rang, and as I opened the front door, I was surprised to see a policeman stood before me. He asked to speak to Gra so I invited him into the lounge. He said he was following up Gra's initial enquiry and wanted to know when we were going to send all the relevant paperwork to the DCI at Taunton Police Station. We said we would take the paperwork along to the police station at the start of the New Year.

A few days into the New Year, we gathered together all the paperwork and took a drive over the snow-covered Quantock Hills to Taunton Police Station. I had driven past the police station many times but, thankfully, never had any reason to enter its doors – until now.

On 4 February 2010, we received a letter from the Detective Chief Inspector at Taunton Police Station stating that a meeting had been arranged in London in mid-February between himself, the Metropolitan Police, the HSE and the CPS, and that he would contact us again after he had attended the meeting. Over the next few months, we were informed by phone that a number of additional meetings had also taken place, but we were never informed of the outcome of the meetings. On 8 May, we received a letter from Thames Valley Police saying the papers in relation to Ben's death had been passed from Avon and Somerset Police to them and that they were in the process of reviewing them. They added that they would consult with the HSE, CPS and RAF Police to try and determine the most appropriate way forward.

We didn't hear from them again for a couple of months, until we received a letter from Thames Valley Police Headquarters dated 10 August 2010. The letter stated that Thames Valley Police 'must decline to conduct an investigation into this case' and 'have concluded that there is no onus on Thames Valley Police to conduct any further investigation'. They added that 'any investigation conducted by the civil police is likely to encounter such significant barriers as to render it ineffective'. A copy of a letter from Thames Valley Police to Avon & Somerset Constabulary also accompanied the letter they had sent to us. In our copy of the letter, Thames Valley Police stated in one of the paragraphs that 'as the Coroner recorded verdicts of accidental death and concluded his inquest, there is no onus on Thames Valley Police to conduct any further investigation'. However, the Coroner did not record verdicts of accidental death, but recorded a narrative verdict.

We felt that as the decision by Thames Valley Police

had been based on incorrect information, then there was a possibility that if they used the correct information, it may have resulted in the end decision being quite different. With our line of thought being so, Gra telephoned Thames Valley Police and informed them that they were wrong when they stated the Coroner had recorded verdicts of accidental death. To Gra's astonishment, he was told that it was us that were wrong and the verdict was one of accidental death. Try as Gra did, he was not able to convince the woman from Thames Valley Police that we were right and she was wrong, even though he informed her that he had the relevant paperwork in front of him. Gra wondered whether the verdict had been recorded incorrectly at the Oxford Coroner's Court so decided to telephone them to inquire. The lady who answered the telephone listened carefully to what Gra had to say then checked the information against the court records. She then confirmed that Gra was quite correct when he said the verdict was a narrative one, and not one of accidental death. Interestingly, she also added that prior to his telephone call, she had also received a call from Thames Valley Police asking the same question.

In their letter to us, Thames Valley Police had offered to meet with us, if we so wished, to explain the reasoning behind their decision. As their letter contained such an important discrepancy, together with other points in the letter we wanted more clarification on, we decided to accept their offer to meet with us. A few days later, Gra contacted them by telephone and informed them that we would like to meet with them in order to understand better how their decision had been reached. During the phone conversation with Gra, the officer informed him that she and a colleague would certainly meet with us, but added and repeated that whatever we said at the meeting would not change the decision they had already made. She said she wanted to make that quite clear to us. We were not entirely surprised by her remark, bearing in mind Gra's earlier discussion with her regarding the inquest verdict. However, we did consider it at odds with the ethos of a modern day police force. Gra and I felt their visit was simply to pacify us, rather than coming with an open and enquiring mind to see whether we might have any information that may be of use to her in an investigation. Despite what appeared to us to be a very negative attitude over the telephone, we were eager to speak with them in person, so an appointment was duly arranged.

On the afternoon of their visit, the two officers from Thames Valley Police arrived at our address at the same time as an officer from the RAF Police. They parked their two cars a little way along from our house and the three of them stood outside in the street talking for a short while. As Gra and I watched them through the window of our front room, deep in conversation, we had an uneasy feeling that their collaboration didn't bode well for us. With their preliminary meeting over, and possibly a strategy agreed, the three of them finished their outdoor conversation and presented themselves on our doorstep. I have to admit, I let them into our house with a certain amount of displeasure.

Prior to their visit, Gra had contacted a number of knowledgeable people in order to go through the points of the police rejection letter and to receive much appreciated advice in advance of the meeting. When the three of them had taken their seats, Gra began by going through each of the points in the police letter that they had used for reasons not to investigate.

It soon became obvious to both Gra and me that no matter what we said, our police visitors were not going to be changing their decision. Some of the reasons they gave for their decision was: the requirement to establish, beyond reasonable doubt, the cause of the crash; the complexity of the common law as applied to corporate and gross negligence manslaughter in these circumstances; confused and conflicting witness testimony; imperfect witness recollections and incomplete documentary evidence; and, finally, the fact that some witness testimony was adduced to the Haddon-Cave inquiry on the understanding that it was to learn lessons. The police added that they had consulted with their legal services team regarding this case, and Gra and I both thought they also said they had contacted the Home Office as well.

A week or so after their visit we received another letter from Thames Valley Police explaining in more detail how they came to their decision. We were adamant that the police had told us that, in considering their reply to us, they had first contacted the Home Office for advice. We pondered over this fact for a couple of months, wondering why they would need to contact the Home Office and what the discussion might have been. Eventually, at the end of October or the beginning of November 2010, we decided to put in an FOI (Freedom of Information) to request the content of the conversation between Thames Valley Police and the Home Office. About ten days after we had submitted the request, Gra received a telephone call from Thames Valley Police who wanted to know why we had submitted the FOI. Gra explained to them that we didn't understand why they needed to contact the Home Office, and having puzzled over the question for a couple of months, we had decided to request the conversation that we believed took place between Thames Valley Police and the Home Office. However, before Gra received a reply from the FOI, he received another telephone call from Thames Valley Police who told him that they had not contacted the Home Office and said they did not understand why we thought they had. The conversation went backwards and forwards, with the police denying that they had told us they had spoken to the Home Office and Gra asking why would we write to the Home Office if their name had not been mentioned in the discussion. In the end, the only solution was for us all to agree to disagree.

Gra also asked the police if it would be possible for us to see a copy of the advice given by the Crown Prosecution Service (CPS) to Thames Valley Police. However, in reply to the question, Thames Valley Police stated in their letter of October 2010, '...the CPS has asked me not to disclose further the advice they have given in this case'. I will add, however, that in the same letter they did admit and apologise for the mistake they made regarding the coroner's verdict.

For us, this was just another obstacle in our long and continuing fight for an element of justice for Ben. However, any sort of justice seemed to be slipping further and further into the unreachable distance.

13

The Health and Safety Executive

Shortly after the findings of the Nimrod review had been released at the end of October 2009, Gra contacted the Health and Safety Executive in London. He wanted to know if they would conduct an investigation into safety matters relating to Nimrod XV230. He was told that, due to the extent of our enquiry, he would need to contact the Deputy Chief Executive at the HSE, Bootle. So, on 13 November 2009, Gra wrote a lengthy letter to the Deputy Chief Executive asking him to investigate in the light of *The Nimrod Review* findings and pointed out some of the many failings that had been highlighted in the *Review*.

Just under a month later, we received a reply from the HSE, dated 3 December 2009, stating that the matters we raised in our letter were complex in both practical terms and in the law. The letter went on to say that the HSE hoped to write to us again early in the new year after they had time to consider the legal and policy implications and to read *The Nimrod Review*. We did not think a reply from the HSE should take too long to arrive as we, maybe naively, expected them to be familiar with the findings of *The Nimrod Review*. After all, they were mentioned in the 'Acknowledgements' page of the *Review*.

The next letter we received from the HSE was dated 10 February 2010. In this letter, the Deputy Chief Executive reiterated the legal and policy implications and mentioned a meeting on 11 December 2009, which was attended by representatives from the Metropolitan Police, the Crown Prosecution Service, the RAF Police and the HSE. He said that, given the complexity of the matters arising at the December meeting, a further meeting was planned for mid-February when the Director of Service Prosecutions for the three armed services would also be attending, as well as representatives from the Avon and Somerset Constabulary. He ended the letter by saying that he would write to us again in early March when he hoped to give us a more detailed response.

As March came and went, with no sign of a letter from the HSE, so too did April, May, June and July. In August 2010, having not heard from the HSE since their letter in early February, Gra eventually decided to telephone them. On doing so, he was informed by a secretary that the Deputy Chief Executive was out of the country on business but she would pass our message on to him when he returned. So again we waited, and as late summer began to creep into early autumn, we had still not received the letter that we were told we would receive in March. As September arrived, still with no sign of a letter or any contact from the HSE, Gra telephoned them again. This time the secretary informed Gra that they were aware we were still waiting for a letter, but the Deputy Chief Executive was a very busy person and hopefully he would be sending a letter to us the following week. I don't like it when someone uses the excuse that they have not done something because they are too busy doing other work. I interpret that as being told my enquiry is unimportant – and the wrongful death of my son is certainly very important to me. The man may be busy, but in my opinion, he is paid to be so; being busy is part of his job and should be managed effectively.

Again we waited for the letter to arrive the following week, and again it did not. Before we knew it, September had turned into October, and still no sign of the *March* letter nor an acceptable reason why it was so late. When the RAF liaison officer had visited us on the 4th of October, he was surprised we had still not received a letter from the HSE as he had been told it was on its way to us. However, we found it slightly unsettling that he should know that the HSE had sent us a letter before we knew. Gra and I also got the feeling that the liaison officer knew the contents of the letter.

On 8 October, Gra phoned the HSE again and spoke to the personal assistant of the Deputy Chief Executive. He was told again that the Deputy Chief Executive would be writing to him and he would receive the letter the following week. This time, seven months after the letter should have been received by us, Gra replied that he would not hold his breath for it, and just as well because yet again it didn't arrive!

Seven months late, on Saturday 16 October, our long awaited HSE letter eventually arrived, and it contained disappointing news for us. I think it was more distressing for Gra than it was for me as I had anticipated the outcome for some time, while Gra remained hopeful that action would be taken by the HSE. I knew, through my own working experience, that a letter with a negative decision takes much more time and precision to write than a letter with a positive decision. 'Yes' is easy to say, but the ramifications of saying 'No' can be far-reaching and complicated unless thought through carefully.

The letter stated that a health and safety investigation would be unlikely to obtain sufficient admissible evidence for there to be a realistic prospect of a conviction against any person, and even if this was not the case, in some cases a court will not allow a prosecution to continue if it decides that it would be unfair for the defendant to be tried because it would amount to an abuse of process. It continued that the HSE had been advised that, for a number of reasons, a court could decide that it would be an abuse of process to bring a prosecution. These included: the time that would have elapsed before any prosecution could be brought; the fact that the Ministry of Defence, being a Crown body, could not be prosecuted; and the fact that there have been three previous investigations into the circumstances of the loss of Nimrod XV230.

The Deputy Chief Executive of HSE concluded by offering to meet with us to talk through the issues addressed in his two-page letter. We decided immediately that we should agree to such a meeting, but first of all, we needed time to digest this most disappointing outcome. In the meantime, Gra decided to email the letter to a solicitor that he'd had previous contact with and who had been extremely good to us in the past by helping us understand some of the many legal issues that the loss of Nimrod XV230 had raised. We also agreed we needed a day or two to come to terms with this most discouraging response from the HSE.

In the evening, as we both sat in the lounge watching the television, Gra suddenly said, "I just need some time to come to terms with their decision."

"I know you do," I replied. And with that, we both began to cry.

Gra said that, by not being able to get a successful prosecution, he felt he had let Ben down, but I assured him we certainly had not let him down. In my opinion, others may have let him down – the RAF may have let him down, the police may have let him down, the HSE may have let him down, and BAE Systems may have let him down – but we had certainly not let him down. Absolutely not! We had done more than anyone else had done in an attempt to get some sort of justice for Ben, and if there was any sort of life after death and Ben was *out there* somewhere, he would know that we had done our very best for him. Yes, I suppose it could be said that we failed, but at least we tried.

It took us a couple of weeks to come to terms with the fact that the HSE would not investigate further, but when we had accepted the situation, we did contact the secretary of the Deputy Chief Executive to arrange a meeting with him. In his latest letter to us, he had offered to talk through the issues that led to his decision, and although Gra and I both knew the decision would remain unchanged, we felt we would like to meet with him to discuss how he reached the decision he did. There were a number of points we needed clarification on. One being the fact that Judith Hackitt CBE, HSE Chair, appeared to be travelling around the country delivering speeches in which she was including Nimrod XV230 an example of what can happen when complacency sets in.

Gra and I could not understand that if the Nimrod XV230 case was so infamous that it warranted public abhorrence, then surely there was a place for the HSE to investigate:

It is absolutely fundamental that we prevent catastrophic events from taking place. Many of you will be familiar with a number of very serious incidents that have happened around the world in recent years – Texas City, Buncefield, the Nimrod crash... Some of these major incidents have already been fully investigated; others are still the subject of on going inquiry and investigation. (Safety Reps' Conference, Birmingham – 17 November 2010)

Many of you will be familiar with a number of very serious incidents that have happened around the world in recent years – Texas City, Buncefield, the Nimrod crash... By drawing together the lessons from events such as the Columbia space shuttle disaster, Texas City and the Nimrod Inquiry... (Safety Rep's Conference, Aldermaston – 16 November 2010)

And recent events provide a stark reminder of why a proactive and dynamic approach is so important. Mercifully, catastrophic incidents happen rarely. This fact, however, can cause a dangerous and insidious level of complacency to develop that can lead to ill-informed strategic decision making. This has been seen repeatedly as a contributory factor in a number of major accidents and was again most recently highlighted as a significant factor in the 'Nimrod Inquiry Report', which I'm sure you are all familiar with. (Devonport Dockyard – 24 June 2010)

Thankfully, catastrophic events happen rarely. This fact, however, can cause a dangerous and insidious level of complacency to develop that can lead to ill-informed strategic decision making. This has been seen repeatedly as a contributory factor in a number of major accidents and was again most recently highlighted as a significant factor in the 'Nimrod Inquiry Report'. (Speech to Babcock International – 6 May 2010)

After much thought and consideration, we decided to send an email to the Deputy Chief Executive suggesting we travel to Bootle to meet with him, but he replied by saying he would come to Somerset and visit us at home if we so wished. With my work and our childcare duties, his offer appeared to be a much better option and so was gratefully accepted by us. After some discussions, a date was arranged to suite everyone and we duly awaited for the day to arrive.

In between arranging the HSE visit and the date of the visit, one of the other relatives from the Nimrod crash heard about our meeting and asked if she could attend, and we of course said yes. She had supported us over the years, and her son and Ben had been friends at RAF Kinloss; the pair had spent off duty time together on outdoor pursuits.

Monday 7 February 2011 at 2.30pm was the date and time of the HSE visit, and although I knew their decision not to launch an investigation would remain unchanged, we felt they had not been as abrupt, intransigent or negative as, in my opinion, Thames Valley Police had been. On the morning of the HSE visit, Gra and I had plenty of time to sit and ponder over the afternoon meeting. As usual, Gra was far more positive about the forthcoming meeting than I was; I knew we were not going to be able to persuade the HSE to rethink their decision, nor come up with a solution that we would find acceptable. As the morning succumbed to the afternoon, the Deputy Chief Executive of the HSE arrived at our house a few minutes early. He had brought with him a legal advisor, and as they both sat themselves down on our sofa, I thought to myself how tiring our continued struggle for justice was. Surely justice should be a right, yet here we were fighting an uphill struggle against the authorities who, it seemed to us, didn't want to upset major defence contractors or use their limited resources on an investigation that might affect their working relationship with those companies.

As we began to talk, I decided I would offer everyone a cup of tea or coffee, not really an unusual task to undertake in the circumstances, but when Thames Valley Police had visited the house, I was so unimpressed with them that I decided not to offer them a drink at all. Not very polite of me, I know, but their manner upset me and I didn't feel I owed them anything, not even a cup of tea.

Once everyone had a drink in front of them, I sat down

and joined in the conversation. I said I didn't understand why the HSE would not begin an investigation into certain companies and their practices, which were responsible for the safety of Nimrod aircraft, when the head of HSE was travelling around the country giving speeches in which she held up the Nimrod crash as an example of a *major accident and a very serious incident.* Missing my point, on purpose I suspected, the HSE man said if mentioning Nimrod in her speeches was upsetting to us, then he could ask her not to mention Nimrod again in any further talks. I raised my eyes to the sky and very gently shook my head from side to side in disbelief at his response.

Gra talked to him about the findings in *The Nimrod Review* by Charles Haddon-Cave QC and the HSE man did concede, saying that by reading the *Review* the conclusion could be drawn that health and safety regulations may had been breached. It was also said in conversation that *The Nimrod Review* had a greater effect on the MOD than a Crown Censure would, and that an investigation with a view to bringing a prosecution could get in the way of an investigation to bring better practices, which was considered not to be a good outcome. What I understood was being said at that meeting with the HSE was that Ben's life, and any justice for taking his life, could be sacrificed for the bigger picture. I wondered what Ben would have thought of it all!

Before the two visitors left our house, we understood that the Deputy Chief Executive of the HSE would be returning to his office and would write to us again when he'd had time to digest what we had said that day. However, we never heard from him again.

14

The RAF Police Investigation

It had been over four years since Ben was killed, and I didn't have much confidence in any action being taken against anyone in relation to the crash of XV230 and Ben's death. However, I certainly didn't consider that a reason to abandon our attempts. As Ben's parents, we felt we had a responsibility to him to explore every avenue in an attempt to obtain a degree of justice for him – no matter how difficult it may be.

The RAF Police were told to investigate the RAF personnel who were named in *The Nimrod Review* by Charles Haddon-Cave QC. They started their inquiry in the months following the publication of the *Review* but had to put their investigations on hold following our representations to the civil police and the Health and Safety Executive. When both those organisations decided that they would not be taking any action against anyone, the RAF Police resumed their inquiries.

Although one of the first people to visit us from the RAF Police regarding the investigation appeared polite and knowledgeable, I still lacked any optimism of anyone being held accountable for the dreadful incident on 2 September 2006 in Afghanistan. After we had welcomed him into our house and invited him to sit down, he began to explain to us how his investigation would proceed. He told us that it would involve a considerable amount of work and, therefore, would certainly not be a quick process. However,

Gra and I had come to realise that already, for nothing regarding investigating Ben's death and the circumstances surrounding it had ever been quick. But we would not have wanted things to have been done quickly, as often things done quickly are not done properly. But it would be right to say that we had not expected the various investigations to take as long as they did.

Along the way, I have wondered whether the slowness of the many meetings and investigations regarding the loss of XV230 were a deliberate attempt to wear us down in the hope that we would eventually give in and just walk away. I realised that we may never see any action brought against anyone named in *The Nimrod Review* but I didn't see that as a reason to quit. Every so often, members of the press would telephone us and want to know if we felt justice had been done now that our compensation claim had been settled. We always answered 'No', for in our opinion, no amount of compensation could equal justice. For us, justice will only have been done when those people responsible for the death of Ben have been held to account.

The RAF man stayed for a number of hours and explained to us the three levels of charges that were available to the RAF when considering the circumstances of the case. We understood these to be: a) dereliction of duty; b) loss of an aircraft; c) loss of an aircraft leading to loss of life. I thought at the time, we would have done well if we managed to get someone to court on the first charge. I couldn't see how, in this case, if there was enough evidence to charge someone for loss of an aircraft, it wouldn't automatically follow that they were also responsible for the loss of life on that aircraft. However, I didn't pick up any confident vibes from our RAF visitor with regard to that matter, and I certainly had my doubts of obtaining a successful prosecution.

It was about two weeks later when the second person from the RAF Police came to visit us. He was the sergeant who was going to be leading the investigation. He explained the investigation process to us and took a statement from Gra that fitted neatly on an A4 piece of paper. I thought how tidy it looked now it was written down on paper, in stark contrast to how are lives had been since Ben was killed. And, again, I didn't foresee an agreeable outcome. The third person to visit us from the RAF Police was the man who had been allocated to us as our liaison officer. A pleasant enough person whom I felt had a somewhat odd role in all of this – however, not as odd as the role the gentleman from Victim Support had. Gra and I certainly found it strange being officially classed as a 'victim' four years after the incident. As with his previous two colleagues, the liaison officer explained that his role was to keep us informed about how the investigation was developing and to take any enquiries we had and pass them on to the relevant people.

The second visit from the liaison officer took place about two weeks after we were first introduced to him. The day before this second visit, the *Mail on Sunday* had printed an article about the amount of compensation the families were going to receive as their solicitors had now reached an agreement with the MOD solicitors. We had not been aware of the article until someone from the *Sunday Times* telephoned us late on the Saturday evening, wanting to know if the story was correct. We hadn't been prepared for the article to raise so much interest on the Sunday it was printed. However, the following day, we seemed inundated with media telephone calls all wanting our view on the content of the article, even though it did not in any way relate to us. It was perhaps unfortunate for the liaison officer that his second visit was the day after the article had been printed, and as I opened the front door to him, Gra was again answering yet another telephone call from someone from BBC Radio. The liaison officer asked me if we'd had a good weekend, and I was abruptly honest with him and said

"No". I then proceeded to explain to him what the previous two days had been like for us. As soon as Gra had finished his conversation, he joined us in the lounge. The liaison officer explained that the purpose of his visit was to obtain a victim impact statement from me which I had to sign in his presence. I had previously prepared the statement, typed it on the computer then emailed it to him. He then had to write it out in longhand and had brought it with him for me to read and sign it.

After that was complete, I showed him a Sunday newspaper article that stated a well-known female singer was going to be flying out to Afghanistan to sing for the troops. Over the years, many pop stars and celebrities have gone to Afghanistan to entertain the troops, but whenever I have asked if it is possible for me to go, the answer has always been "No, it is still too dangerous." So this time, I had kept the newspaper article and gave it to the liaison officer to pass higher up the command chain. I just could not accept the reason I was always given when celebrities seemed to have no problem going out to Afghanistan. The liaison officer said he would refer my request/complaint further, but I knew nothing would come of it. Since Ben's death, I have found it difficult that we were unable to see his body or visit the place he was killed. Usually, relatives can do either one or the other, and often both. But we haven't been able to do either. Pop stars and celebrities often make the long journey to Afghanistan, but as a bereaved mother whose son was killed serving his country, it feels as if I am just not considered important enough.

The article in the *Mail on Sunday* had generated a lot of interest and, understandably, the local newspaper had printed a similar story in their weekly paper. As I work locally, I have never really liked articles appearing in our local newspaper as we are a quiet, private family who just want to get on with our lives with as little fuss as possible.

However, because of Ben's very public death, we have become the subject of many media articles in our quest for accountability, but with that also came gossip and criticism from a small number of people who really did not know the whole situation at all, and at times that has been upsetting for me.

We were also concerned that we had not heard from the Health and Safety Executive for many months, so Gra asked the liaison officer if he could find out when we could expect to hear from them. The liaison officer left our house a few hours after his arrival, taking with him the signed statement and a few questions. On Monday 11 October 2010, Gra received a telephone call from the liaison officer. He said that the Squadron Leader was away, but he had spoken with his next in line and raised our concerns with him. He added that he was surprised we had still not received a letter from the Health and Safety Executive; we were not.

It was not until early November that Gra received a further telephone call from the RAF Police, stating that the lead police officer had left and another would be taking over. He added that letters explaining the investigation would be sent out to all the families on Monday 15 November and that we would also be receiving a copy.

Christmas came and went, our fifth without Ben, and that time of year was always a poignant reminder of what we had taken from us. In the second week of the New Year, while I was babysitting our twin grandchildren, Thomas and Poppy, Gra received a telephone call from the RAF liaison officer. He told Gra that his telephone call was just to update us with how the investigation was going, and to let us know that they would shortly be interviewing four people who attended the IPT meetings with regard to the safety case and that they expected to get all four interviews done within the next four weeks. Gra's hopes were raised by this latest bit information, but again mine were not. I had come to realise over the years that justice was not going to prevail. Now I just needed to learn to *live* with that fact.

On a cold winters afternoon in 2011, we received another telephone call from the RAF liaison officer. He explained to Gra that a meeting had been arranged for the following day between the RAF investigating team and their equivalent at the Crown Prosecution Service (CPS). He informed Gra that the RAF investigating team would be explaining to the legal people the details of the interviews that they had been carrying out and discussing whether further statements were needed from other people. Gra asked him if he had any idea how long the investigation might take and was informed that they were unable to provide a possible time scale today, but after the following day's meeting, they may know more. To end the conversation, the liaison officer said to Gra that he understood the Deputy Chief Executive of the HSE was coming to visit us.

At the end of the dialogue, Gra replaced the receiver then relayed the conversation to me. I was annoyed to hear that the RAF Police knew the HSE man was coming to visit us before we had been told, for I did not understand what business that was for the RAF Police. Although I was cross, I was also upset. I know I shouldn't have been, because after four and a half years of trying to achieve an element of justice, I should have been used to, what appeared to me to be, a sharing of information between some of the organisations.

A few hours later, and still distressed and annoyed, I telephoned the liaison officer and ended up crying down the telephone to him as I tried to relay the total unjustness I felt about the whole debacle. I told him about the woman from the HSE and how she travels around the country referring to the Nimrod crash as an example of a 'very serious incident' and extremely bad practice at the very least, yet her department still does not take any action against those responsible. As my frustration built and waned, it was eventually replaced by a feeling of despair and helplessness, and after our conversation had ended and I had thanked the liaison officer for listening to me, I sat and cried. How could fourteen people be killed in an aircraft accident and yet no one be interested in taking any action against those responsible? Yes, it was an accident, but as *The Nimrod Review* revealed, it was an accident that could and should have been avoided.

The following day, while I was at Andy and Deborah's house looking after Poppy and Thomas, the liaison officer telephoned again and spoke to Gra. He said the meeting earlier that day had gone well and further interviews were being arranged. He asked Gra how I was feeling and said he was sorry I was so upset the previous day.

A little while later, in the middle of February 2011, we received a totally unexpected telephone call from an investigative journalist asking us if there were any on going investigations regarding Nimrod XV230. He said he had been informed by an anonymous source that a court decision had been made that overturned the Haddon-Cave decision to provide immunity from prosecution for people that were interviewed during the Nimrod review. Gra told him that we hadn't heard about such court action but explained to the journalist that it did correspond with the current RAF investigation.

After an interesting conversation, the journalist said he would contact us again if he heard further information. After his conversation had ended, Gra decided to telephone the RAF liaison officer, even though by this time it was late evening, to enquire if he knew of any such court action or similar decisions. The liaison officer said he wasn't aware of any decisions of this kind but would make further enquiries the following day and let us know. As we had not heard back from him after two days, Gra decided to telephone him again, but the liaison officer said that he still had no knowledge of any action suggested by the investigative journalist.

On the morning of 9 March 2011 and amidst his child-minding duties, Gra answered the telephone to the RAF Squadron Leader who was at the head of the investigation. The telephone call was to update us on the stage the investigation had reached. Gra was told that the interviews had been completed and the paperwork was shortly to be sent to the RAF's equivalent of the CPS, who would decide whether any court action was to follow. Gra was also told that one of the people being investigated had taken early retirement a couple of months ago. This meant if any court action was going to be taken against that person, then it had to be instigated within six months from him leaving the RAF – again more bad news, but not unexpected.

A week later, we received a letter from the RAF Police. It said that they thought there may be sufficient evidence to support a charge against a former head of the Nimrod Integrated Project Team for failing to check the accuracy of the NSC. The charge being considered was of 'Signing a certificate relating to aircraft belonging to Her Majesty without having ensured its accuracy', and comes under Section 50 of the Air Force Act 1955. Gra was disappointed at the low level of the charge being considered, but at least there was a glimmer of hope that someone may be held accountable for their actions.

Some months later, on a dull summer's day in the middle of July, we were both surprised to take delivery of a letter from the Service Prosecuting Authority (SPA), RAF Northolt. Although we had been waiting for the letter for many months – and even years if we considered how long it had been since Ben was killed – its arrival still sent a sudden shock wave through our bones. I opened the letter tentatively, fearful of its contents and their significance and weary with nearly five years of fighting for accountability and justice for Ben. The letter explained in 587 words why the SPA would not be bringing a prosecution against anyone in relation to the crash of Nimrod XV230 and all on board. Sadly, the contents of the letter were of no surprise to me, and were actually what I had been expecting from the beginning of the RAF Police investigation. Gra, understandably, was very disappointed. He had considered the RAF to be an honourable service that respected honesty and high principles and always hoped that, in the end, justice would prevail. But it was not to be.

At the beginning of August 2011, the head of the RAF police investigation came to visit us at home and explained why the SPA felt they could not take the investigation any further. He told us he was not surprised with the decision, having spent the best part of a year going through all the information and relevant paperwork. He said they had met many difficulties trying to obtain witness statements, and also statements from people who had worked at one of the companies named in *The Nimrod Review*. Although he considered there to be enough evidence to show an offence had been committed, the referral chain was said to be complicated due to the officer being such a senior figure.

I understand the file was referred to the RAF at High Wycombe, and although it could have been dismissed immediately, it was referred upwards to the Services Prosecution Authority. They read the information provided by the Investigation Branch and also listened to the recording of the taped interviews. However, we were told that throughout the process of the taped interviews, the officer in question replied 'no comment' to every question he was asked. In my opinion, if you have nothing to hide, then there is no need to say 'no comment' to every question. Our RAF visitor said the officer being interviewed had a right to silence as everyone does when being interviewed for a criminal investigation.

At the end of the taped interviews and on his way out of the office, we were told that the interviewee began to say that he really *would* have liked to answer the questions, but at that point, his solicitor stepped in and told him that that was enough and he must not say anything more because it would just be written down in the notebooks of the investigating team. He did, however, present the investigating team with a short prepared written statement before he left in which, we were led to believe, he said that he did now realise that he was given inaccurate information by one of the other people named in *The Nimrod Review*.

To obtain a realistic chance of a conviction, the investigating team were told by the SPA that they needed to provide more statements. But when they contacted people asking if they would give a statement to them that could be used in court, nearly all of them answered 'no'. People were prepared to give interviews for the Nimrod review because they had been promised that the information they gave would not be used in disciplinary proceedings against the individual who gave it, unless there was evidence of gross misconduct. However, this investigation was different and there was no promise of immunity from prosecution. Therefore, people who had spoken to investigators for the Nimrod review were not prepared to speak to the RAF Investigations Branch. One key person initially agreed to speak with them, but a short while later, said on reflection he had now changed his mind.

I understand a number of BAE employees were contacted by the Investigations Branch by letter, by telephone or with a visit, but very few replied. Of those that did reply, we were told that they each provided identical letters, stating that they didn't wish to help in the investigation. In a statement by BAE Systems on 29 October 2009, they acknowledged 'that there were a number of failings in [their] application of [their] internal processes and procedures during the course of work undertaken as part of the Nimrod safety review which took place between 2001 and 2004'.

We were also informed by the RAF Investigator that another of the problems that faced them during their inquiries was the poor documentation of paperwork within the IPT. He said that the terms of reference to tell them what their jobs were were out of date and not signed. So it was difficult to know what their responsibilities were because no one had signed anything. He added that, while it can be brought out as a criticism in a public enquiry, because the administration was poor and because there was a lack of paper records, it would be very difficult to conduct a successful criminal prosecution. With regard to the safety case, he said they knew the job had not been done properly but they could not gather the evidence to prove it because it largely didn't exist. He added that one of the problems was that it is harder to prove beyond reasonable doubt someone has not done something, (for example, read the *Nimrod Safety Case*) than to prove that somebody has done something.

From his conversation with us that day, Gra and I were led to believe that there were many things wrong within the system, but with people's reluctance to be interviewed by the RAF Investigations Branch, the evidence was not available to them. He mentioned also a general reluctance from some of the former members of the IPT to be interviewed. Before the man from the RAF Investigation Branch left our house and our lives for the last time, he did leave us with the impression that, had everyone involved been prepared to provide a full and frank testimony, the outcome may have been very different.

15

Life Without Ben

Life without Ben... Sometimes it is still difficult to say those words. Maybe because he is in my thoughts every single day. Framed photographs of Andy, Matt and Ben are around the house so I see them every day, I will just never see Ben in person again. As parents of three children, Gra and I are proud of each and every one of them. Over the years, they have all experienced their own difficult times and come through them as stronger, compassionate and more understanding individuals.

Ben's death left a huge void in all our lives that is going to stay with us for as long as we live, and there is no getting away from that fact. It's something we have to incorporate into our present lives and manage it as best we can – and as a family, we do that. But the pain is always there. It doesn't really go away. Over the years, and with the help of many months of counselling, I have learnt to accommodate that pain, as I'm sure the rest of the family have. I have compartmentalised it neatly within my thoughts, and after much struggling over the years, I feel I can now say I have an element of control over it. I would say the majority of people I meet as I go about my everyday life do not detect my pain at all and that is how it should be. But it is still there, lurking just below the surface and ready to pounce at any moment if I should weaken.

But it is true to say life does go on. At the very beginning of this long and devastating journey, on 2 September 2006, life did suddenly come to an abrupt halt for all the family. Very slowly and painfully we have picked up the pieces we've been left with, and we continue with our lives until our time is also up.

A lot has happened within the family since Ben's death. Babies have been born, marriages have taken place and, sadly, also a separation. Ben has missed all of these experiences, having had them taken from him by those responsible for the un-airworthy RAF aircraft he was flying in. I think he would have been delighted and surprised by the marriages, but understandably disappointed by the separation. He would have been absolutely delighted to have become an uncle to our four lovely grandchildren, Callum, Charlie, and twins Poppy and Thomas. The eldest, Callum, was born just three months after Ben's death, and Callum was one of the reasons I was inspired to write this book. At the time of Ben's death, I found it so heartbreaking that he and Callum missed knowing each other by just three months. However, he does have Benjamin as his middle name. I wanted to redress that miscarriage of justice for Callum, and any future grandchildren. So, although they would never have the privilege of meeting their Uncle Ben, they would be able to read about him and know how much all the family love and miss him.

I think it is fair to say that when Ben died, a part of us all died with him. But Gra and I have lovely memories of our time spent with our son that will remain with us for the rest of our lives, as I know the others in the family do also. We very much enjoyed all the times we visited him and his fiancée in the cold and blustery highlands of Scotland, and now find solace as we return to those places each year.

We particularly remember the times we travelled to the town of Forres, Morayshire, along the single-track railway and waiting at the station for Ben to collect us. Although he would say he'd be there to meet us as we stepped off the train, he was usually a few minutes late. As Gra and I stood on the station platform awaiting his arrival and breathing in the tranquillity of the area, he would suddenly appear, driving hurriedly into the station car park and coming to an abrupt halt beside us. He would then fling open his car door and greet us with a big smile and an even bigger hug. And that was Ben. Even now, five years after his death, we still find passing Forres Station exceptionally difficult because of those happy times, now transformed into memories. And thankfully there are many, many more memories to match that one, all of them bringing us joy and tears as we continue our lives without Ben.

I would like to say more about those people who refused to be interviewed by the RAF Police and their Special Investigations Branch, and also those that, when interviewed, replied 'no comment' throughout. Unfortunately legal restraints bar me from doing so, but they will have to live with their consciences for the rest of their lives.

Occasionally, I think about the last flight Ben took on 2 September 2006, and wonder whether at any time during those final few minutes did he think he was going to die and, more importantly, was he scared. I really hope the answer to both those questions is 'no'.

I began writing this book over five years ago, when I was very much a victim. As victims, Gra and I have attended a number of services held in respect of our servicemen and women killed in Afghanistan, and each November on Remembrance Day, a number of our family attend the service in our hometown of Bridgwater where Ben's name is poignantly displayed on the War Memorial in King Square. I didn't attend the service this year as I find it too distressing, but Gra and Matt went together. I stayed at home and looked after Matt's two young children, Callum and Charlie. However, Gra and I are both beginning to feel that we have attended sufficient memorial services over the last five years to warrant our withdrawal from future ones. I find them very draining and they just serve to keep me in the 'victim' role, a label which I am trying to free myself from. And I don't need an a pre-arranged service in order to remember Ben, for I think about him every single day and will continue to do so for the rest of my life. Nowadays, I like to think of myself more of a survivor than a victim.

I will end with the final paragraph of an article I had printed in the *Mail on Sunday* supplement, in August 2009, which remains relevant to this day:

> *Today's RAF servicemen and women are hopefully flying in much safer aircraft than they were before September 2 2006, and for that I am pleased. But that improved safety has come at a very high cost to many families. It has been paid for by Ben's family, his fiancée and others close to him, with our loss and continuing grief at losing such a treasured and loved person. But ultimately, the cost of ensuring these aircraft are now safe to fly has been paid for by Ben, with his blood and with his life, and that should never be forgotten.*

Passing out ceremony, RAF Cranwell

Top: Ben, Graham and Trish at a family wedding

Left: Ben fresh out of the shower

Ben 6 weeks before his death, laying decking at his new house

Ben, Matt and Andy, July 2006

Memorial for Crew 3 Nimrod XV230 at RAF Kinloss

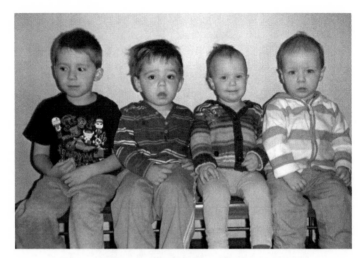
The Knight grandchildren, Callum, Charlie,
and twins Poppy and Thomas, April 2011

Acknowledgements

Writing this book has been a long and, at times, painful process and I would like to thank the following people for their help and support:

My husband Graham for his love and patience
Also my two surviving sons:
Andy for his objective criticism and his literary input, especially in the technical parts, and Matt for his understanding and unconditional acceptance of this project whilst experiencing his own difficult times.

Also to Callum, Charlie, Poppy and Thomas whose presence has inspired me over the years to keep writing; Helen Hart at SilverWood Books, for her help in realizing the publication of the book; David Hill for his invaluable advice, knowledge and support on all matters of airworthiness; Irwin Mitchell Solicitors, for their legal representation and help regarding the Inquest; John Cooper, for all his support and legal advice; Jimmy, for all his support, practical knowledge and friendship over the years, and especially for the kindness he extended to me as we sat together in the pub in Forres while I cried.

Bibliography

The Nimrod Review
Charles Haddon-Cave QC ISBN 978-0-10-296265-9

Transcript of BBC Panorama Programme
On a Wing and A Prayer shown Monday 4 June 2007
www.news.bbc.co.uk/1/hi/programmes/panorama/6724095.stm

The Dambusters
John Sweetman, David Coward and Gary Johnstone
ISBN-10: 0316726184 / ISBN-13: 978-0316726184

Tigress Productions (Makers of the *Dambusters* Series)

The Big Table Film Company (the *Dambusters* Series)

www.pprune.org

www.e-goat.co.uk

Board of Inquiry into the accident involving Nimrod
MR2 XV230 – www.mod.uk/DefenceInternet/
AboutDefence/CorporatePublications/BoardsOfInquiry/
BoiNiBoiNim2Xv230.htm

The 5 Stages of Grief
Elizabeth Kubler-Ross

Goodbye Dearest Holly
Kevin Wells

Sara Payne – A Mother's Story
Sara Payne

Top Gun
Paramount Pictures

Extracts from speeches by Judith Hackitt CBE, HSE Chair
www.hse.gov.uk/aboutus/speeches/hse-chair.htm

Chronology Of Events

Sept 2 2006 – RAF Nimrod MR2 XV230 explodes following an on-board fire, all 14 crew killed.

Sept 13 2006 – Repatriation Ceremony at RAF Kinloss as the 14 bodies were flown home.

Nov 17 2006 – Ben's funeral takes place at Inverness Crematorium.

Dec 4 2006 – The crew of a Nimrod MR2 used a teapot to block a hatch gap in their plane after a mid-air mechanical fault.

Jan 29 2007 – Memorial Service at RAF Kinloss.

Feb 22 2007 – All UK military Nimrod MR2 aircraft grounded as a precautionary measure after a routine safety check uncovered a dent in a fuel pipe.

March 18 2007 – *The Times* newspaper reports:
RAF rebels quit over fuel danger in ageing spy plane. E-mails from RAF flight crew allege that Nimrod spy planes are being kept airborne despite repeated problems with fuel leaks such as the one suspected of causing the deaths of 14 servicemen.

Nov 8 2007 – The *Telegraph* newspaper reports:
Fresh doubts were cast over the safety of the RAF's Nimrod MR2 surveillance aircraft fleet after it emerged that a plane put out a Mayday call over Afghanistan when crew discovered fuel pouring into the bomb bay.

Dec 4 2007 – Board of Inquiry releases its findings. The Defence Secretary makes a Statement in the House of Commons saying: "It is clear to me that some of the findings of the board of inquiry identify failings for which the Ministry of Defence must take responsibility. On behalf of the MOD and the Royal Air Force, I would like to say sorry for those failings to the House, but most of all to the families of those who lost their lives."

May 7 2008 – Inquest begins at Oxford Coroners Court.

May 23 2008 – Oxfordshire Coroner returns a narrative verdict stating he will make rule 43 recommendations to the MOD: "I have given the matter considerable thought and with the age of the aircraft at the forefront of my mind I see no alternative but to report to the Secretary of State for Defence that the Nimrod fleet should not fly unless, and until, the ALARP standards are met."

May 23 2008 – The Secretary of State for Defence announces he will not ground the aircraft.

March 9 2009 – The BBC reports that all Nimrod MR2 aircraft that have not had a vital safety modification are to be grounded by the Ministry of Defence

March 31 2009 – Nimrods based overseas withdrawn in order to replace engine bay hot air ducts.

Oct 26 2009 – *The Nimrod Review* publishes its findings. He stated that: "My Report concludes that the accident to XV230 was avoidable, and that XV230 was lost because of a systemic breach of the Military Covenant brought about by significant failures on the part of the MOD, BAE Systems and QinetiQ. This must not be allowed to happen again."

March 26 2010 – the Nimrod MR2 was finally withdrawn from service.

Oct 17 2010 – the RAF's new Nimrod reconnaissance planes, the MRA4 (meant to replace the old Nimrod MR2s), grounded over safety worries.

Oct 18 2010 – *The Strategic Defence and Security Review* is announced, cancelling the MRA4; all 9 Nimrod MRA4 aircraft are to be dismantled.

Jan 27 2011 – Nimrod MRA4, which cost taxpayers more than £4bn, dismantled and turned into scrap.

Lightning Source UK Ltd.
Milton Keynes UK
UKOW050712090312

188643UK00001B/15/P